MEETING WITH
JESUS
THROUGH THE
BIBLE
AND FINDING YOUR
LIFE
IN HIM

Heino A. Blaauw

ISBN 978-1-63814-932-3 (Paperback)
ISBN 978-1-63814-933-0 (Hardcover)
ISBN 978-1-63814-934-7 (Digital)

All Scripture quotations are taken from the English Standard Version (ESV) translation of the Bible unless specifically denoted otherwise.

Covenant Books, Inc.
11661 Hwy 707
Murrells Inlet, SC 29576
www.covenantbooks.com

To Finn, Hudson, Tessa, Mila, and Henry
The unfolding of your words gives light; it imparts understanding to the simple (Ps 119:130)

To all lovers of the Living Word who breathes eternal life from the pages of the Sacred Script

FOREWORD

It was October 2005, and I was invited to teach something from the Bible to classes of seminary students at Onesimus Nesib Seminary in Aira, western Ethiopia. I was there through an invitation from a friend, Dr. Carl Toren, who has a long-standing relationship with Aira Hospital and Nursing School where he has served both full-time and then intermittently in medical missions since 1988. The hospital and seminary are located adjacent to each other.

Meeting the students, I rejoiced in their eagerness to learn the Scriptures. Relative to North American seminary students, their knowledge of the Bible was limited but certainly growing. As part of our three-week mission trip, Dr. Toren and I brought each of them an NIV Study Bible. They were preparing to become pastors in a region where the Christian faith was rapidly growing. It is common for these students upon graduation to pastor three to five churches in circuit-ministry.

Assessing their needs, I determined that it would be most helpful for these students to gain a unified understanding of the Bible. Upon initial encounter, the Bible presents very disparate types of writing—history, law, poetry, gospel, epistle, wisdom, prophetic, and apocalyptic literature. Sixty-six books composed over the course of 1,500 years by forty different authors—what unites this compilation of writings?

There are various answers to that question, each important. One is to look at the overarching movement of the Bible from creation to fall to salvation to new creation. Another is to look at the unifying theme of the covenants that God enters with humankind from the Adamic covenant through Noahic, Abrahamic, Mosaic, Davidic, and into the New Covenant. Yet another unifying theme to the Bible is that of the kingdom of God—how and where God's reign is manifest in the ages of history, each manifestation revealing significant truth to live in toward the full restoration of creation.

Of all these options, there is yet another unifying theme to the Bible, one which I contend is the most important of all. That theme is the person and life journey of Jesus Christ. As the introduction to this book explains, Jesus claimed that all Scripture points to Himself. More than that, He stated that the purpose of Scripture was to draw people to Himself that they might have true life in Him (John 5:39–40).

This then became the course that I taught those Ethiopian seminary students, and now, upon further development, has become this book. Unpacking the life story of Jesus, I sought to teach those eager students how the Bible foreshadows or explains the person and work of Jesus. But this was not only done for the sake of biblical coherence; it also was done to nourish their spiritual life through Scripture, that they might meet with Jesus in their reading and study. More than that, this life story of Jesus, the Christ plotline, is also descriptive of salvation, of a person's journey in Christ. Understanding this plotline therefore gives wisdom and pastoral counsel for the Christian life.

In 2005, that course was received by those Ethiopian students with enthusiasm and joy, thanks be to God. It not only nourished their biblical understanding, it strengthened their own life in Christ and their ministry to others. May God use this book to those same ends in your life.

—Heino A. Blaauw, January 2021

CONTENTS

INTRODUCTION

Scripture's Interpretive Key

As they were talking about these things, Jesus himself stood among them, and said to them, "Peace to you!" But they were startled and frightened and thought they saw a spirit. And he said to them, "Why are you troubled, and why do doubts arise in your hearts? See my hands and my feet, that it is I myself. Touch me, and see. For a spirit does not have flesh and bones as you see that I have." And when he had said this, he showed them his hands and his feet. And while they still disbelieved for joy and were marveling, he said to them, "Have you anything here to eat?" They gave him a piece of broiled fish, and he took it and ate before them.

Then he said to them, **"These are my words that I spoke to you while I was still with you, that everything written <u>about me</u> in the Law of Moses and the Prophets and the Psalms must be fulfilled."** (emphasis mine) Then he opened their minds to understand the Scriptures, and said to them, "Thus it is written, that the Christ should suffer and on the third day rise from the dead, and that repentance for the forgiveness of sins should be proclaimed in his name to all nations, beginning from Jerusalem. You are witnesses of these things. And behold, I am sending the promise of my Father upon you. But stay in the city until you are clothed with power from on high." (Luke 24:36–49)

Imagine being there! The Risen Jesus manifesting Himself bodily, confirming the glory of His resurrection. Then after eating with them, He trains His followers how to read the Bible. He opens their minds to understand it. He trains them so that after His bodily ascension into the heavenly realm, His ongoing spiritual presence could be received through the Scripture.

> Everything written about me in the Law of Moses and the Prophets and the Psalms must be fulfilled. (Luke 24:44)

Jesus "opens their minds" (v. 45) to begin to realize that the central principle of biblical understanding is its witness to His person and life. The purpose of this book is to help you join with these disciples in that Jerusalem class. It is to help you gain an understanding of the Bible which Jesus Himself had, namely, an understanding that draws you into knowledge of and fellowship with the Risen Lord Himself.

That is why a Christian reads the Bible. Earlier in His ministry, Jesus had chastised the Jewish religious leaders for not reading the Bible through this lens.

> You search the Scriptures because you think that in them you have eternal life; and it is they that bear witness about me, yet you refuse to come to me that you may have life. (Jn 5:39–40)

Might we be under the same charge? Does your Scripture reading lead you into fellowship with Jesus? Scripture can be read for a host of valid reasons—to gain moral precept, to enjoy poetic beauty, to learn ancient history, to contemplate a great story. Yet none of these reasons attain Scripture reading's highest purpose which is to draw you into life with Christ and in Christ.

This then is the interpretive key of Scripture. Christians wear the spectacles of the person and life of Jesus when we read Scripture, for Jesus' life is the messianic life, the *saving* life, the *kingdom* life, the *eternal* life that we are called to know and trust and enter for our salvation. In Jesus' life, a Christian finds their identity, calling, and hope. Paul writes,

> For me to live is Christ and to die is gain. (Phil 1:22)

All of Scripture is given to nourish us in that eternal life, the kingdom which is and is to come.

How then can we best be drawn to Jesus through Scripture? That comes through discerning the movements of the plotline of His life. Jesus alluded to this plotline on the day of His resurrection when He manifested Himself to two disciples walking the road to Emmaus. Not recognizing his presence, He began to reveal Himself to them through the Bible.

> And he said to them, "O foolish ones, and slow of heart to believe all that the prophets have spoken! Was it not necessary that the Christ should suffer these things and enter into his glory?" And beginning with Moses and all the Prophets, he interpreted to them in all the Scriptures the things concerning himself. (Luke 24:25–27)

Through suffering to glory is the core plotline of Jesus' life. But in more detailed fashion, the movements of His life can be broken down as follows:

- Beginnings—from eternity past, miraculous conception by Word and Spirit, special birth

11

- Call/Favor
- Vision and Ministry
- Learning Obedience
- Suffering
- Death/Bearing Judgment
- Resurrection
- Ascension
- Reign
- Return/Final Judgment
- Reunion
- Future Glory/The New Creation

As Jesus made clear, each of these movements of His life is witnessed to in Scripture. In the Old Testament, they are witnessed to prophetically. In the gospels, they are enacted in the testimony of His life. In the rest of the New Testament, they are explained, and their implications worked out for Christian faith, identity, obedience, and hope. Jesus unifies the Bible. Reading it calls us to life in Him.

To that end, it helps to think of the flow of Jesus' life as a *plotline*. A typical literary plotline has a *beginning* (introduction, setting, characters, problem issue—i.e., Cinderella, the neglected stepdaughter); *rising action* (series of events where issues become more complicated and conflict increases—i.e., the Prince seeks a bride and calls for a ball); *climax* (where a significant breakthrough occurs—i.e., the Prince falls in love with Cinderella at the ball); *falling action* (resulting action from the climax—i.e., the Prince searches for his love with the glass slipper); *conclusion* (resolution of the story—i.e., the Prince and Cinderella live "happily ever after").

This type of plotline is typically graphed in this fashion:

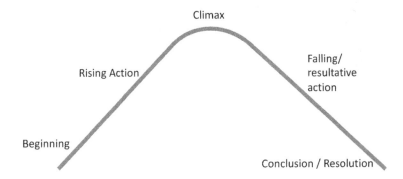

However, because Jesus' plotline moves downward into the climax of the suffering and death of His crucifixion, it is more helpful to graph the movements of His story in inverse fashion:

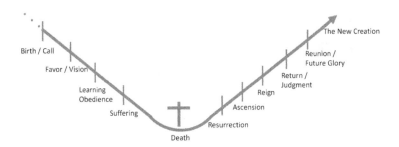

The purpose of this book is to instill this "Christ plotline" deeply into your understanding, not only for the sake of reading Scripture but even more for the sake of your identity as a Christian. Jesus' life is to be discerned from all the pages of Scripture and then embraced, through repentance and faith, as one's identity unto salvation.

We read the Scriptures to know Jesus, put our life in Him, to fellowship with His Living Presence, and to become part of His kingdom purposes.

CHAPTER 1

The Story of Joseph

Read Genesis 30:1–24, 37–47

To further embed this Christ plotline into our understanding, let's look at the story of Joseph from the book of Genesis. Undoubtedly, Jesus had a special affinity for this story because in it, more fully than any other individual biblical story, He could see His messianic identity, calling, vision, suffering, and future glory. It is a story that foreshadows Jesus' life and highlights many of the constituent movements of our plotline. Therefore, it is profitable to review them before exploring each individually.

Favor with the Father

The key to understanding the Joseph story is the favor he has with his father, Jacob. This favor found expression in Joseph's "coat of many colors."

> Now Israel loved Joseph more than any other of his sons, because he was the son of his old age. And he made him a robe of many colors. (Gn 37:3)

A moralistic reading of Scripture would chastise Father Jacob for having favorites. No good father parents his children that way! But this misses the crucial Christocentric point of the story. The reason behind Jacob's favor toward Joseph is the messianic promise that God gave to Jacob's grandfather, Abram. In Genesis 12, God promised Abram that through his family line, He would bring salvation and blessing to this world.

> And I will make of you a great nation, and I will bless you and make your name great, so that you will be a blessing. I will bless those who bless you, and him who dishonors you I will curse, and in you all the families of the earth shall be blessed. (Gn 12:2–3)

Through Abram's seed, God would again make this world as He intended it to be. Jacob understood his own life in the context of this family calling (it's why he sought his elder brother's birthright), and he identified his son Joseph to likewise be the spiritual leader in this identity. For that reason, he bestowed favor on Joseph.

Why Joseph and not any of his other ten brothers? (Benjamin later inherits this favored identity when Joseph is supposedly dead.) This is on account of Joseph being the firstborn of Rachel, Jacob's primary love. His birth is long-awaited and, like many of the "messianic births" in Scripture, it comes after a period of barrenness. It is a *special birth* (even involving mandrakes, a purported fertility aid [Gn 30]!). Upon his birth, this firstborn of Rachel is named Joseph, meaning "may he add." Jacob is confident that the family's Abrahamic promise, identity, and spiritual calling is going to be fulfilled through this son, hence, the favor.

This unique "favor of the Father" is, of course, central to Jesus' messianic identity. He is the "beloved of God," words spoken at His baptism and transfiguration.

> This is my beloved Son with whom I am well pleased. (Mt 3:17, 17:5)

Later in His ministry, Jesus declares,

> Truly, truly, I say to you, the Son can do nothing of his own accord, but only what he sees the Father doing. For whatever the Father does, that the Son does likewise. (Jn 5:19–20)

A Christian's salvation comes

> to the praise of God's glorious grace, which he has freely given us in the One He loves. (Eph 1:6 NIV)

Joseph's favor with his father within the Abrahamic promise of salvation foreshadows Jesus' favor with His heavenly Father.

Vision

That favor of a father leads to vision! With Dad for me, the future is bright! Joseph becomes a dreamer, a divine dreamer. In Genesis 37:5–11, Joseph envisions his brothers bowing before him, acknowledging him as their ruler, and then he has a second similar dream, this time including his mother and father bowing before him.

Father Jacob is intrigued by these dreams (v. 11), undoubtedly on account of God's Abrahamic promises to his family.

Considering all the messianic promises that God would raise up a ruler on earth (Is 9; Ps 2, 110), how could Jesus not see His own identity in those Joseph dreams? Surely, He did, though He handled that understanding more maturely and obediently than did Joseph. Jesus realized that it was through servanthood (Mk 10:45) that He would receive the "name that is above every name."

> That at the name of Jesus every knee should bow in heaven and on earth and under the earth, and every tongue confess that Jesus Christ is Lord, to the glory of God the Father. (Phil 2:10–11)

Suffering

This unique favor and vision led to Joseph's sufferings. On account of jealousy, his own brothers reject him (Gn 37:11), cast him into a pit, sell him into slavery—a slavery that brings him out of the land promised to his family to Egypt, far from his father.

What motivated the religious establishment of Jesus' day to reject him? Pilate knew.

> For he knew it was out of envy that they had handed Jesus over to him. (Mt 27:18 NIV)

Further, it was in response to Jesus' own claims to a unique identity with His Father that His own brothers turn on Him. When Jesus claimed, "I and the Father are one" (Jn 10:30), the Jews picked up stones to stone Him.

Is Jesus truly a unique human being? Does He share in a unique love with the Father, a unique love from the Father, a unique love unto the Father? And is that love part of God's saving purposes to restore the world? These are the central questions of the Bible, and these are the questions upon which individual human histories pivot. These questions again arise later in the Joseph story.

Learning Obedience

God's saving purposes for Joseph, and through him for our world, do not end on account of his rejection and sufferings. In fact, they are furthered through them because Joseph learns obedience in his time of separation from the father. He is sent to Egypt and becomes a servant in Potiphar's household (Gn 39). There he gains maturity and wisdom. He learns how to administrate and lead the affairs of Potiphar's household. There, too, he faces temptation in the person of Potiphar's wife. But not forgetting his identity in God (v. 9), Joseph resists temptation and remains obedient. Joseph's obedience is preparing him for his future greater calling.

Describing Jesus, Hebrews 5:8–9 states,

> Although he was a son, he learned obedience
> through what he suffered. And being made per-
> fect, he became the source of eternal salvation to
> all who obey him. (Heb 5:8–9)

In learning obedience, Jesus eventually becomes our Great High Priest (Heb 4:14) and Ruler who will lead all the affairs of God's household in this age.

> For we do not have a high priest who is unable
> to sympathize with our weaknesses, but one who
> in every respect has been tempted as we are, yet
> without sin. (Heb 4:15–16)

Death

Despite resisting temptation and remaining obedient, Joseph is treated unjustly and cast into prison. Potiphar's wife falsely accuses him (Gn 39:16–18), and Potiphar himself (did he, knowing his wife, think that Joseph was actually innocent?) has him put into prison. Joseph is "numbered with the transgressors" (Is 53:12) and is

> put into the prison, the place where the king's prisoners were confined. (Gn 39:20)

There are many such "deaths"—exiles, flights, pits, and prisons—throughout the witness of Scripture. Jesus knew of them and, through their witness, foretold His own death (Mk 8:31) as He lived the messianic life and destiny.

Resurrection/Ascension

That messianic destiny, foretold in Joseph's life, goes from prison to palace! While in prison, Joseph continues his journey of obedience through "death" and becomes a person through whom destinies are determined and mankind divided. He meets the cupbearer and baker of the king of Egypt (Gn 40). Each has dreams which Joseph, through the strength of his fellowship with God (v. 8), interprets. One is restored to his ministry with the king; the other was hung on a tree.

Jesus divides.

> Do not think that I have come to bring peace to the earth. I have not come to bring peace, but a sword. (Mt 10:34)

A sword severs and divides.

More significantly and again with the help of God, Joseph interprets the dreams of the Pharaoh of Egypt (Gn 41). This leads to Joseph's "resurrection and ascension." Pharaoh's dreams foretell a period of abundance and then famine, a famine which requires wisdom to cherish and store the produce of the years of abundance. (Might this abundance allude to the years of Jesus' obedience on earth which becomes bread for the famine of our age?)

Joseph not only interprets Pharaoh's dreams but also recommends that he

> look for a discerning and wise man and put him
> in charge of the land of Egypt. (Gn 41:33 NIV)

Joseph has become that discerning and wise man through his sufferings and obedience. Therein, he is resurrected from prison and ascends to the "right hand" of the almighty King Pharaoh.

The parallel to Jesus' life is straightforward. His glorification in the resurrection and ascension is nothing less than His coronation as Ruler of this age (Ps 2). He is seated at the right hand of God Almighty (Ps 110, Heb 1:13). He is the man of "discernment and wisdom" and through Him, God is building His reign on earth.

Reign

The reign of Joseph for the sake of the glory of Pharaoh is succinctly told. Through his prudence, Joseph literally becomes the "bread of life" for the world.

> So when the famine had spread over all the land,
> Joseph opened all the storehouses and sold to the
> Egyptians, for the famine was severe in the land
> of Egypt. Moreover, all the earth came to Egypt
> to Joseph to buy grain, because the famine was
> severe over all the earth. (Gn 41:56–57)

This ministry of Joseph brings honor to Pharaoh. In return for food and seed, Joseph acquires the world's livestock and land, tribute and service to the glory of Pharaoh's name (Gn 47:13–25).

> And they said, "You have saved our lives; may it
> please my lord, we will be servants to Pharaoh."
> (Gn 47:25)

This reign is testimony to the glory of the Messiah's reign.

> For to us a child is born, to us a son is given, and
> the government will be on his shoulders… Of the
> increase of his government and peace there will
> be no end. He will reign on David's throne and
> over his kingdom, establishing it and upholding
> it with justice and righteousness from that time
> on and forever. The zeal of the Lord Almighty
> will accomplish this. (Is 9:6–7 NIV)

The reign of the ascended Jesus today is the fulfillment of the
Joseph story. He is the Bread of Life (Jn 6:35) to whom we turn in
the famine of our age. He is the nourishment of God's grace and
truth. His obedience is the bread of life—crucified for our reconciliation with God, risen to guide us by His Spirit into lives of obedience
and divine blessing. Jesus is reigning today, bringing the world in
subjection to God. As it is described in 1 Corinthians 15,

> For he must reign until he has put all his enemies
> under his feet. The last enemy to be destroyed is
> death… When all things are subjected to him,
> then the Son himself will be subjected to him
> who put all things in subjection under him, that
> God may be all in all. (1 Cor 15:25–26, 28)

Judgment

In the context of his reign at the right hand of the Pharaoh,
Joseph brings his brothers into judgment. Like the rest of the world,
they must come to him on account of the famine of that day. When
they do come before him, they bow down to him with their faces to
the ground (Gn 42:6). True to the messianic dream/vision, "every
knee shall bow before him and every tongue confess that he is Lord"
(Phil 2:10). His brothers do not recognize that this lord is none other
than their brother, Joseph. He knows them, however, so Joseph tests

his brothers. After determining that his father, Jacob, and younger brother, Benjamin, are yet alive, Joseph designs several tests to gauge the hearts of his brothers (Gn 42–43).

These tests are centered around Benjamin who has now become the favored son of Father Jacob in the light of God's Abrahamic promises to the family line. (Jacob assumes Joseph is dead on account of the testimony of the blood-stained robe [Gn 37:33].) Ultimately, Joseph wants to determine whether his brothers respect and honor the favored son and the unique love of the father for the son—or are their hearts yet jealous and callous to that love?

Therefore, before selling food and seed to his brothers, Joseph immediately imprisons them on the charge that they are spies. Upon their release, he then insists that one of the brothers remain imprisoned until they return with their youngest brother. The brothers' response is encouraging to Joseph. Among themselves, they remorsefully recognize this chastisement as originating in their previous mistreatment of Joseph (Gn 42:21–22). They are owning up to personal guilt in the rejection of the *beloved son*. Their hearts have indeed begun to change, and it moves Joseph to tears (v. 24).

When famine persists, and Benjamin eventually arrives in Egypt (to the chagrin of Jacob), Joseph ramps up his testing. He concocts a scheme (Gn 44) whereby Benjamin is forced to remain in Egypt, apart from his father, and become a slave to Joseph. How will the brothers respond? Will they simply discard Benjamin and return to Canaan, discarding him as they had earlier done to Joseph? Or will they honor the beloved son in the light of God's promises to their family line?

Their response, led by Judah, brings them salvation. They would all give themselves to be slaves to Joseph (v. 16), owning their previous guilt in his mistreatment. Further, they honor the unique love of Jacob for Benjamin.

> We cannot go down. Only if our youngest
> brother is with us will we go. We cannot see the
> man's (Jacob's) face unless our youngest brother

> is with us... Our father's life is closely bound up
> with the boy's life. (Gn 44:26, 30 NIV)

Judah then lays down his life (Gn 44:33) for the sake of the love
of the father for the beloved son. This response again brings Joseph
to tears, and he reveals himself to his brothers (Gn 45).

Judgment for all mankind will ultimately come down to this
same test. How will you respond to the unique love of the Father and
the Son made manifest in the person of Jesus?

> The Father loves the Son and has given all things
> into his hand. Whoever believes in the Son has
> eternal life; whoever does not obey the Son shall
> not see life, but the wrath of God remains on
> him. (Jn 3:35–36)

Reunion and the New Land

Understood in the light of its messianic witness, there is hardly
a more moving scene in all of Scripture than when Joseph makes
himself known to his brothers.

> Then he threw his arms around his brother
> Benjamin and wept, and Benjamin embraced
> him, weeping. And he kissed all his brothers and
> wept over them. (Gn 45:14–15 NIV)

Even more moving is Joseph's reunion with his father, Jacob,
when he, too, comes to Egypt.

> As soon as Joseph appeared before him, he threw
> his arms around his father and wept for a long
> time. Israel said to Joseph, "Now I am ready to
> die, since I have seen for myself that you are still
> alive." (Gn 46:29–30 NIV)

Joseph is Jesus with whom one day Christians will be fully united. He will make Himself known to His brothers.

> Beloved, we are God's children now, and what we will be has not yet appeared; but we know that when he appears, we shall be like him, because we shall see him as he is. (1 Jn 3:2)

Upon reunion, Joseph settles his father and brothers into the region of Goshen. It is the "best part" of all the land of Egypt (Gn 47:6, 11).

> No eye has seen, no ear has heard, no mind has conceived what God has prepared for those who love him—but God has revealed it to us by his Spirit. (1 Cor 2:9–10 NIV)

Thus, it was in the Spirit that the apostle John

> saw a new heaven and a new earth, for the first heaven and first earth had passed away...and heard a loud voice say, "Now the dwelling of God is with men, and he will live with them. They will be his people, and God himself will be with them and be their God. He will wipe every tear from their eyes. There will be no more death or mourning or crying or pain, for the old order of things has passed away...and the glory and honor of the nations will be brought into it." (Rv 21:1, 3–4, 26 NIV)

"I go to prepare a place for you" (Jn 14:3) in this new earth, Jesus said to his disciples on the eve of His crucifixion, death, and resurrection. When Joseph revealed himself to his brothers, he declared,

> God sent me ahead of you to preserve for you a remnant on earth and to save your lives by a great deliverance. (Gn 45:7 NIV)

Joseph is Jesus foretold. After Father Jacob dies, his brothers are again uncertain about their fate—were they truly forgiven for their rejection and mistreatment of the beloved son? Joseph said to them,

> Don't be afraid...you intended to harm me, but God intended it for good to accomplish what is now being done, the saving of many lives. I will provide for you and your children. (Gn 50:20 NIV)

What fellowship with Jesus can be had through the Joseph story! Can you imagine what it meant to Him as He read and reflected on it while growing into His messianic identity? Certainly, a lot!

And perhaps this Joseph story was one of the scriptures that Jesus used to "open the minds" of His disciples on that Resurrection-Day evening when He "explained to them the things written about Him in the Law of Moses, the Prophets and the Psalms" (Luke 24:44–45). The Joseph story foretells Jesus' messianic identity, vision, suffering and death, resurrection and ascension, reign and reunion, even His promise of a new land for the people of God! In one story, it describes the Christ plotline (see introduction) that we now want to go into in more detail, for *all* Scripture bears witness to Jesus' life.

More than that, this plotline bears witness to a believer's life in Christ. What's true of Jesus becomes true for those "in Christ." In this, the Bible not only bears witness to Jesus, it likewise bears witness to a Christian's life *in Him*. Paul writes,

> I have been crucified with Christ. It is no longer I who live, but Christ who lives in me. And the

life I now live in the flesh I live by faith in the
Son of God, who loved me and gave himself for
me. (Gal 2:20)

Like Jesus, each Christian experiences a miraculous birth with
divine calling, favor, and vision. Each Christian must learn obedience, even through seasons of suffering. Each Christian knows death
and resurrection, spiritually now and physically later. Each Christian
is resurrected to serve God in this age in the anointing of Jesus Christ
who reigns as prophet, priest, and king. All of this is done in preparation for the future resurrection, judgment, and reunion with the
Lord, after which we live in His glory in the new earth and heavens.

So let's now explore each of these movements of the Christ plotline that we might recognize their witness in all Scripture, name
their testimony to Jesus' life, and then be strengthened in our own
life in Christ. The Old Testament bears witness to the Christ life; the
Gospels describe that Christ life in the person of Jesus; the rest of the
New Testament either explains and applies that Christ life (the letters) or reveals its growth and future in the ever-expanding kingdom
of God on earth (Acts/Revelation). The Biblical references to each of
these aspects of the Christ plotline in the following chapters are not
meant to be exhaustive but suggestive, so that the reader sees more
clearly that plotline in Scripture and history, living within it.

CHAPTER 2

Divine Birth and Call

The Christ Plotline

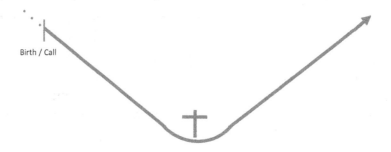

Birth / Call

Conception

Jesus' life on earth begins with a miraculous conception through God's Word and Spirit.

> The angel (Gabriel) said to Mary, "Do not be afraid. You have found favor with God. You will be with child and give birth to a son."… "How can this be," asked mother Mary, "since I am a virgin?" The angel answered, "The Holy Spirit will come upon you, and the power of the Most

High will overshadow you. So the one to be
born will be called the Son of God." (Luke 1:30,
34–35 NIV)

Every Christian can readily relate to Mary. Truly the life of
Christ in us involves a miraculous conception through the agency of
God's Word and Spirit.

For you have been born again, not of perishable
seed, but of imperishable, through the living and
enduring word of God. For, "All men are like
grass, and all their glory is like the flowers of the
field; the grass withers and the flowers fall, but
the word of the Lord stands forever." And this is
the word that was preached to you. (1 Pt 1:23–25
NIV)

That "word" Peter writes of is the same eternal Word that
became incarnate for our salvation (Jn 1:14) and dwells in us by the
power of His Spirit.

Christ in you, the hope of glory. (Col 1:28)

This Word births our beginning on the Christ plotline of eternal life.

Further, being the eternal Son of God, Jesus' life predated His
conception in the womb of Mary (pictured in the three dots above).

Jesus said to them, "Truly, truly, I say to you,
before Abraham was, I am." (Jn 8:58)

So, too, are the origins of the Christian's new birth actually
"dated" in the eternal counsels of God. As Paul writes,

Blessed be the God and Father of our Lord Jesus
Christ, who has blessed us in Christ with every

spiritual blessing in the heavenly places, even
as he chose us in him before the foundation of
the world, that we should be holy and blameless
before him. (Eph 1:3–4)

Old Testament Foreshadowing

In order to best see the foretelling of Jesus' miraculous conception (and a Christian's in Him), it is helpful to expand our understanding of the "emptiness" of Mary's barren, virgin womb. Yes, that
conception was quite directly foretold in Isaiah's famous prophecy:

> Therefore the Lord himself will give you a sign.
> Behold, the virgin shall conceive and bear a son,
> and shall call his name Immanuel. (Is 7:14)

But more broadly than this, Jesus' miraculous conception is
seen in the emptiness of Scripture's stories of infertility and despair,
of chaos and darkness, of judgment and death, even of humility and
repentance. It is into these "wombs" that the eternal life of Christ is
conceived by God's Word and Spirit.

There are numerous stories of infertility in the Bible. Rachel's
with Joseph was described in the previous chapter. More well-known
is the story of Sarah's infertility and barrenness, the wife of Abraham.
God had promised them a son through whom the world would be
blessed.

> Then Abraham fell on his face and laughed and
> said to himself, "shall a child be born to a man
> who is a hundred years old? Shall Sarah, who is
> ninety years old, bear a child?" (Gn 17:17)

For that reason, God declared that the son born to them would
be named Isaac, meaning "he laughs."

Another prominent story of barrenness is Hannah's in 1 Samuel
1. She turned to the Lord in her despair, praying in the temple with

such fervency that the priest Eli thought she was drunk. Through his word (v. 17) God brings life into Hannah's womb. With her husband, she bears a son, Samuel ("asked of God"), who becomes a great prophet and leader among God's people, foreshadowing Jesus' ministry. Likewise, the life of the deliverer and judge, Samson, begins with a special birth story (Jgs 13). So, too, does the life of Obed (meaning "servant of God"), born to Ruth and, indirectly, to the sonless, barren Naomi.

Moses' birth story broadens our understanding of the emptiness into which new life comes. As an infant, he was "cast upon the waters" of the Nile River in the context of Israel's despair and miraculously raised up (Ex 2). New life in Christ meets God's people in the place of chaos and darkness. In the birth of the earth itself, things were first "formless and empty, darkness over the surface of the deep" (Gn 1:2). Then God spoke, and through His Word and Spirit come light and life, order, beauty, and goodness!

The creation of Adam in Genesis 2 also bears witness to the miraculous conception of Jesus, the second Adam. God "breathes" into Adam's nostrils the breath of life, and man becomes a "living being" (v. 7). Biblically, the breath of God is a picture of the Holy Spirit. The first Adam's creation then becomes a foretelling of Jesus—the uniquely "alive" human being, eternal life Himself. Note, too, in the first Adam's creation story that he is put to sleep (death) so that a bride could be formed from his side, even as Christ's bride is taken from the "blood and water" of His "side" in death (Jn 19:34).

Emptiness also comes after scriptural stories of judgment. God sends His people into exile in Babylon as judgment for their sin. It leads them into humility and repentance embodied in the prayers of Nehemiah (Neh 1) and Daniel (Dn 9). Into that context comes the Word of God, bringing new miraculous life from—of all places—the Persian King Cyrus:

> The Lord, the God of heaven, has given me all
> the kingdoms of the earth, and he has charged
> me to build him a house at Jerusalem, which is in
> Judah. Whoever is among you of all his people,

may the Lord his God be with him. Let him go
up. (2 Chr 36:23)

Now certainly this last scriptural witness can also be understood in the pivot of death and resurrection as illustrated along our
Christ plotline. Both the beginning of life in Christ and resurrection
life in Christ are accomplished by God's Word and Spirit. In God's
work, death precedes new life. Ultimately, that new life belongs to
a Christian through the power of Jesus' resurrection. As the apostle
Peter writes,

> Blessed be the God and Father of our Lord
> Jesus Christ! According to his great mercy, he
> has caused us to be born again to a living hope
> through the resurrection of Jesus Christ from
> the dead, to an inheritance that is imperishable,
> undefiled, and unfading, kept in heaven for you.
> (1 Pt 1:3–4)

Whether at the outset of our Christ plotline or in the pivot of
death and resurrection, the fundamental recognition is that the life
of Christ, as witnessed to in Scripture and received by each Christian,
comes first in the context of deadness, barrenness, infertility, humility, and darkness. It requires a divine miracle by the power of God's
Word and Spirit. That is the significance of Mary's womb.

> And you were dead in the trespasses and sins in
> which you once walked, following the course of
> this world, following the prince of the power of
> the air… But God, being rich in mercy, because
> of the great love with which he loved us, even
> when we were dead in our trespasses, made us
> alive together with Christ. (Eph 2:1–2, 4–5)

The context of this entry point into life in Christ is most
encouraging. Regularly, affairs in this age bring us to places of emp-

tiness and chaos. Regularly, believers need to recalibrate their lives along the Christ plotline. It is in the place of humility that Christ's life is born. It is in Bethlehem's manger of repentance and death that new life begins.

> Humble yourselves before the Lord, and He will
> exalt you. (Jas 4:10)

It is in the place of barrenness that we may wait upon the God of new life through Word and Spirit.

> Out of the depths I cry to you, O Lord; O Lord,
> hear my voice. Let your ears be attentive to my
> cry for mercy... O Israel, put your hope in the
> Lord, for with the Lord is unfailing love and with
> him is full redemption. (Ps 130:1–2, 7 NIV)

Call

The birth of Jesus comes with a call to service.

> An angel of the Lord appeared to him (Joseph)
> in a dream, saying, "Joseph, son of David, do not
> fear to take Mary as your wife, for that which
> is conceived in her is from the Holy Spirit. She
> will bear a son, and you shall call his name Jesus,
> for he will save his people from their sins." (Mt
> 1:20–21)

Jesus is *the* Servant of the Lord (cf. Is 40–66). His life, begun in the humility and darkness of a stable, has as its purpose the facilitation of the kingdom of God on earth. That purpose is founded upon the forgiveness of sins and reconciliation of His people with their Holy Creator. That Creator God is the source of all life. Hence, as the Servant of the Lord, Jesus proclaimed Himself to be the "Life" of the kingdom (Jn 11:25, 14:6), the "Vine" (Jn 15:5) in whom to abide to live a fruitful life of service to God.

The Scriptures are replete with stories of God calling people to His service, stories that find their fulfillment in Jesus and those in Christ. Abram was a "wandering Aramean" (Dt 26:5), the son of an idolater (Jn 24:2) when God called him to be His servant. That context was his darkness and humility. That call came through the agency of the Word and Spirit and began him in the life of Christ. Abram then began his journey of faith as a servant of the Lord and father of God's covenant people.

Isaiah's call to be a kingdom servant came through a vision of the holiness of God (Is 6), bringing him into the humility of repentance and ruin. But there the Lord brought forgiveness (v. 6–7) and then asked,

> "Whom shall I send, and who will go for us?"
> Then I (Isaiah) said, "Here am I! Send me."

David's humility is in his position as the eighth and youngest son of Jesse. He is the one anointed by Samuel (1 Sm 16) and called to be Israel's future king. (Note: Often, this Christocentric theme of one called into kingdom service from a place of humility is reflected in the later-born son, i.e., Abel over Cain; Jacob over Esau; Perez over Zerah [Gn 38]; Ephraim over Manasseh; David over Saul. These later-born servant sons point to Jesus, the "second Adam" [Rom 5, 1 Cor 15:22]. They also point to sinful humanity's need for a "second birth" in Christ, the new birth of the Spirit [Jn 3:6–7].)

Samuel's servant call came in the darkness of night (1 Sm 3). Ezekiel's came when he lay facedown on the ground before the glory of God (Ez 2). Jeremiah's call in Christ came when he was yet unborn:

> Now the word of the Lord came to me, saying,
> "Before I formed you in the womb, I knew you,
> and before you were born I consecrated you; I
> appointed you a prophet to the nations." (Jer
> 1:4–5)

The nation of Israel's call to be God's light to the world (Is 49:6) also came to them in their context of humility.

> The Lord did not set his affection on you and choose you because you were more numerous than other peoples, for you were the fewest of all peoples. But it was because the Lord loved you and kept the oath he swore to your forefathers that he brought you out with a mighty hand and redeemed you from the land of slavery, from the power of Pharaoh king of Egypt. (Dt 7:7–8 NIV)

One more, Moses' call is particularly instructive as Scripture points us to Jesus' servant call and a Christian's kingdom call in him. It is found in Exodus 3. It comes after the "first Moses" has "died." He had failed as a leader, becoming a murderer. Then fleeing to the desert, he becomes a shepherd. He learns humility (Ex 2). In that context comes his new life in Christ with its servant call. At the burning bush, God calls him by His Word (Ex 3:4), in holiness (v. 5), to know Him (v. 13) and live in dependence upon Him (vv. 11–12):

> "Who am I that I should go to Pharaoh and bring
> the children of Israel out of Egypt?" He (God)
> said, "But I will be with you."

Birth in Christ comes with the call to be God's kingdom servant. Birth in Christ is not merely a spiritual awakening; it is for the sake of extending the rule of God in and through one's personal life. Just as Jesus is the Light of the world (Jn 8:12), in Him, Christians are God's salt and light (Mt 5:13–16). Christians are a people called by God's Word and Spirit in Christ, "out of darkness into his wonderful light" (1 Pt 2:9) and then into service:

> For we are his workmanship, created in Christ
> Jesus for good works, which God prepared

beforehand, that we should walk in them. (Eph 2:10)

More will be written about this call to service in a later chapter on Jesus' ascension reign.

CHAPTER 3

Favor and Vision

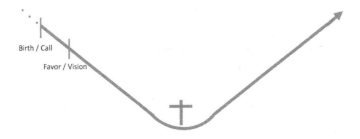

Central to Jesus' self-understanding and ministry is His identity as the "beloved Son" who lives and serves within His Father God's favor. In that favor, He becomes the agent of God's kingdom rule on earth.

> "The time is fulfilled," Jesus said [as he began his public ministry]. "And the Kingdom of God is at hand. Repent and believe in the gospel." (Mk 1:15)

This invitation to enter God's kingdom involves seeing its future on earth, vision gained in Christ, both personally and globally, and then living into it.

Favor

Jesus understood Himself as the beloved son of God from His earliest years of life. Lost by His parents in Jerusalem as a young boy and subsequently found in the Temple, He explained to them:

> Why were you searching for me? Didn't you know
> that I must be in my Father's house? (Luke 2:49)

Thereafter, His growing years are described with this simple statement:

> And Jesus increased in wisdom an in stature and
> in favor with God and man. (Luke 2:52)

Upon entry into public ministry, Jesus was confirmed in this God-favored identity at His baptism:

> You are my beloved Son; with you I am well
> pleased. (Luke 3:22)

Again, later in life with death impending, on the Mount of Transfiguration, Jesus hears that divine declaration:

> This is my Son, whom I love, listen to him! (Mk
> 9:7 NIV)

This identity of Jesus as the uniquely beloved Son living in the favor of God is fundamental to the Gospel of John's presentation of Jesus. Jesus Himself states:

> All that the Father has is mine. (Jn 16:15)

> O righteous Father, even though the world does
> not know you, I know you. (Jn 17:25)

> He who sent me is with me. He has not left me alone, for I always do the things that are pleasing to Him. (Jn 8:29)

> The Son can do nothing of his own accord, but only what he sees the Father doing. For whatever the Father does, that the Son does likewise. For the Father loves the Son and shows him all that he himself is doing. (Jn 5:19–20)

But this unique identity of Jesus in the favor of God should never be understood as status for the sake of privilege. Instead, it is for the sake of service. Through His death and resurrection, Jesus breaks open His life so that His people could enter this identity and live in it.

> Truly, truly, I say to you, whoever believes in me will also do the works that I do; and greater works than these will he do, because I am going to the Father. Whatever you ask in my name, this I will do, that the Father may be glorified in the Son. (Jn 14:12–13)

> The glory that you have given me I have given to them, that they may be one even as we are one, I in them and you in me. (Jn 17:22–23)

Before applying this identity to those in Christ, how is the unique favor of God in the messianic Son prefigured in the Old Testament?

Certainly, Adam and Eve became favored of God through the garments of skin they were clothed in after their fall into sin (Gn 3:21). In that favor, Eve would become the "mother of all the living" (v. 20), through whose seed would come the snake-crushing Messiah (v. 15). Their son, Abel, was looked upon in God's favor too (Gn 4:4) before his death at the hand of jealous Cain. Noah "found favor in the eyes of the Lord" (Gn 6:8) in the context of mankind's extreme wickedness. That favor was evidenced in Noah's righteous life.

> Blameless in his generation. Noah walked with God. (Gn 6:9)

Within the context of God's saving covenant, Abram leads the way as the "beloved of God."

> And I will make of you a great nation, and I will bless you and make your name great, so that you will be a blessing. I will bless those who bless you, and him who dishonors you I will curse, and in you all the families of the earth shall be blessed. (Gn 12:2–3)

Abram's son, Isaac, and then grandson, Jacob, too, share in this messianic anointing. The Lord declares,

> I have loved Jacob, but Esau I have hated. (Mal 1:3, Rom 9:13)

This "divine favor" in the person of Jacob was meant for all of Israel to understand as their identity.

> "I have loved you," says the Lord [of Israel]. (Mal 1:2)

Deuteronomy 7:7–8 adds,

> It was not because you were more in number that the Lord set his love on you and chose you, for you were the fewest of all peoples, but it is because the Lord loves you and is keeping the oath that he swore to your fathers. (Dt 7:7–8)

Isaiah 42:1–2 describes the messianic calling of Israel (which Jesus fulfills):

> Behold my servant, whom I uphold, my chosen, in whom my soul delights; I have put my Spirit upon him; he will bring forth justice to the nations. (Is 42:1–2)

As someone living in God's favor, Moses likewise prefigures Jesus.

> And the Lord said to Moses, "This very thing that you have spoken I will do, for you have found favor in my sight, and I know you by name." (Ex 33:17)

Thus it was, like Jesus, the Lord would speak to Moses face-to-face as a man speaks with his friend (Ex 33:11).

However, of all Old Testament types foreshadowing Jesus' unique favor with God, David stands out. He is the man "after God's own heart, who does everything God wants him to do" (Acts 13:22). In God's unmerited favor (2 Sm 7:18), David is the anointed son and king (2 Sm 7:12–14). In that identity, David lives and prays and trusts.

> The Lord was my support. He brought me out into a broad place; he rescued me, because he delighted in me. (Ps 18:18b–19)

> You still the hunger of those you cherish; their sons have plenty, and they store up wealth for their children. And I—in righteousness I will see your face; when I awake, I will be satisfied with seeing your likeness. (Ps 17:14b–15 NIV)

Numerous psalms attest to David's life of intimacy with God based on his identity of anointed favor. Others even prayed in the "name of that anointing."

> O Lord God of hosts, hear my prayer; give ear, O
> God of Jacob! Behold our shield, O God; look on
> the face of your anointed! (Ps 84:8–9)

How Jesus must have cherished these psalms in His life on earth. His trust in God was nourished by them. Christians are privileged to read them in the same way as they are read in Christ. He is the anointed One through whom God's people have secured His favor.

This favor is at the heart of the gospel! Jesus has come to bring it on earth. He is the Messiah who has come to "proclaim the year of the Lord's favor" (Is 61:2, Luke 4:19). Through Jesus' life, death, and resurrection, the identity of becoming a "beloved son/daughter" is for everyone! As the apostle to the Gentiles, Paul writes,

> God made him who had no sin to be sin for us, so
> that in him we might become the righteousness
> of God. As God's fellow workers we urge you not
> to receive God's grace in vain. For he says, "In the
> time of my favor I heard you, and in the day of
> salvation I helped you." I tell you, now is the time
> of God's favor, now is the day of salvation. (2 Cor
> 5:21–6:2 NIV)

That favor is entered through repentance and faith in Jesus as Savior and Lord. In Him, what's true of Jesus is true of each believer. We become God's beloved children (Jn 1:12), adopted in Christ (Eph 1:5). We are free from condemnation (Rom 8:1), citizens of heaven (Phil 3:20). We are channels of Christ's life (Jn 15:5) and can approach God with freedom and confidence (Eph 3:12). In Christ, we are God's workmanship (Eph 2:10), confident that the good work God has begun in us will be perfected (Phil 1:6). Nothing can separate us from the love of God as His favored ones (Rom 8:35), and all things work together for our good (Rom 8:28).

> He who did not spare his own Son but gave him up for us all, how will he not also with him graciously give us all things? (Rom 8:32)

In this favor of God through Christ, His people find personal value and life's meaning.

Vision

That meaning is best understood in the context of the kingdom of God on earth and a life lived into it. The kingdom—the restored rule of God on earth and the blessings therein—is the great project that Jesus came to formally inaugurate. His foundational message was

> The time is fulfilled, and the kingdom of God is at hand. Repent and believe in the gospel [= good news]! (Mk 1:15)

As it's been succinctly put, "Jesus did not come to bring us to heaven, He came to bring heaven on earth!" (first heard from N. T. Wright, "The Kingdom of Heaven Will Be on Earth," YouTube, May 18, 2016).

The vision of the kingdom of God on earth begins in the Old Testament, particularly with the prophets. In Isaiah 65, the prophet envisions a future age on earth, one in God's shalom—wholeness and healing—

> No more shall there be in it an infant who lives but a few days, or an old man who does not fill out his days (Is 65:20);

43

a kingdom of safety and provision:

> They shall build houses and inhabit them; they
> shall plant vineyards and eat their fruit (Is 65:21);

a world free from violence and destruction wherein work is
meaningful:

> They shall not labor in vain or bear children for
> calamity, for they shall be the offspring of the
> blessed of the Lord... The wolf and the lamb
> shall graze together; the lion shall eat straw like
> the ox, and dust shall be the serpent's food. They
> shall not hurt or destroy in all my holy moun-
> tain. (Is 65:23–25)

In its completion, this kingdom will be the creation of a "new
heavens and new earth" (Is 65:17).

Further, in this kingdom, all nations will "stream to the mountain of the Lord's temple to be taught the ways of the God of Jacob"
(Is 2:1–4, Mi 4:1–3). Thus, the word of the Lord will bring justice
on earth and peace between the nations.

> They will beat their swords into plowshares and
> their spears into pruning hooks. (Is 2:4)

Consequently,

> the earth will be filled with the knowledge of the
> glory of the Lord, as the waters cover the sea. (Hb
> 2:14)

In this messianic kingdom,

> the people walking in darkness have seen a great
> light; on those living in the land of the shadow

of death a light has dawned… For to us a child is born, to us a son is given, and the government will be on his shoulders. And he will be called Wonderful Counselor, Mighty God, Everlasting Father, Prince of Peace. Of the increase of his government and peace there will be no end. (Is 9:2, 6–7 NIV)

Jesus came to both inaugurate and live into this future kingdom of God on earth. He adopted Isaiah's messianic words for His personal mission statement:

The Spirit of the Lord is upon me, because he has anointed me to proclaim good news to the poor. He has sent me to proclaim liberty to the captives and recovering of sight to the blind, to set at liberty those who are oppressed, to proclaim the year of the Lord's favor. (Luke 4:18–19)

Jesus inaugurated God's kingdom through inviting people to enter that kingdom by becoming His followers (Luke 5:1–11). In Jesus, people are justified with God and made fit for entrance to the kingdom. Thereafter, the life of His disciple is to bear witness to the nature of God's kingdom in both character and work. It is to live as a sign of the kingdom, bearing witness to earth's future. This is how Jesus Himself understood His work on earth.

Jesus fed the hungry (Jn 6:1–15), not only to call people to Himself as the Bread of Life (Jn 6:35) but also because in God's kingdom, there is provision for our every need. He healed the sick because in God's kingdom, there is health—no more sickness, no more sorrow. The Gospel of John explains these works as "signs" of the kingdom (Jn 20:30). His works are pointers and witnesses to the kingdom's presence and future fullness. Jesus delivered the demonized because there is no oppression in God's kingdom. That is why

He sets the captive free. In the new earth, each person has dignity and value. In Luke 11:20 Jesus said,

> But if it is by the finger of God that I cast out demons, then the kingdom of God has come upon you. (Luke 11:20)

All of Jesus' work must be understood in the vision of the kingdom of God. He gave sight to the blind both because He is the Light of the World (Jn 8:12) and because in God's future earth, there is enlightenment in God's will—the earth "filled with the knowledge of God" (Hb 2:14). Through Zacchaeus, Jesus restored property to those who had been cheated thereof because in God's kingdom, there are rights of property.

> They shall sit every man under his vine and under his fig tree and no one shall make them afraid. (Mi 4:4)

Jesus raised Lazarus from the dead to both draw people to Himself as the "resurrection and the life" (Jn 11:25) and to point people to a future earth wherein there is no more dying (Rv 21:4), an earth replete with life!

Jesus came to bring heaven on earth.

> In Him all things hold together. (Col 1:17)

He has formally begun the project of reuniting earth with heaven. Through Jesus, God's people enter the kingdom of heaven in their identity (Phil 3:20) and live toward it in character and witness by the power of His Spirit.

Upon her pregnancy with the physical presence of Jesus, Mother Mary caught a vision of this kingdom:

> My soul glorifies the Lord and my spirit rejoices in God my Savior, for he has been mindful of the

humble state of his servant... He has scattered those who are proud in their inmost thoughts. He has brought down rulers from their thrones but has lifted up the humble. He has filled the hungry with good things but has sent the rich away empty. (Luke 1:46–55 NIV)

In God's kingdom, the virtue of humility is extolled. God's people live into it.

When the Holy Spirit of Jesus was unleashed at Pentecost, Peter explained His impact upon the people of God, grounding it in Joel's prophecy:

And in the last days it shall be, God declares, that I will pour out my Spirit on all flesh, and your sons and your daughters shall prophesy, and your young men shall see visions, and your old men shall dream dreams. (Acts 2:17)

The Spirit brings kingdom dreams and kingdom visions to those who are in Christ.

Those visions start with one's character. In Jesus, we meet the character of God on earth as human. He is the "image of the invisible God" (Col 1:15). To become Jesus' disciple is to fall in love with this character and aspire to grow toward it. The Spirit anoints the people of God with vision in that journey.

For those whom he (God) foreknew he also pre-destined to be conformed to the image of his Son, in order that he might be the firstborn among many brothers. (Rom 8:29)

In salvation, one is enchanted with the person of Christ, the true human—His humility, His courage, His trust, His compassion, His forgiveness, His wisdom, His self-control, His joy, His honesty, His love. In response, the Holy Spirit brings a believer into the longing of repentance. Repentance is the sorrowful acknowledgment of the ways that one's own character is less than and other than that of Jesus'. Repentance, therefore, is grounded in the vision of God in Christ and is ultimately hopeful because until a person can see himself as a better, bigger, truer, more heavenly person (through meeting Jesus), there is no moving toward that character. Repentance then is a lifelong journey in this age for the follower of Jesus. In fact, the deeper and more comprehensive one's character of repentance grows, the more hopeful a believer can be on that day when the fullness of Jesus in glory is revealed. Yes, measures of Christian character growth do occur in this age as we "walk in step with the Spirit" (Gal 5:25), but more telling of a believer's reward in future glory is the life of repentance. Repentance forms vessels to contain the glory of Christ. The deeper and broader those vessels are formed, the more of the glory of His character will they hold on that future day when He is fully revealed.

But Christian vision is not confined to character. Spirit-born kingdom vision pours into all of life. It extends to "every square inch" of creation (Abraham Kuyper). Like Jesus Himself, the vision of God's shalom kingdom on earth energizes a believer's work and witness.

As foretold in the first covenant, the kingdom of God encompasses society and land. Israel's laws moved their society toward the justice and mercy of God's kingdom. Relative to neighboring nations in their day, those laws valued the dignity of all people. That preparatory covenant, too, cherished the "promised land." And in the fullness of God's new covenant in Christ Jesus, the "new earth" is promised to God's people (Mt 5:5).

Consequently, the Spirit of Christ leads people into this vision of God's shalom kingdom. It is a kingdom of health (so Christians have begun hospitals); provision (Christians feed the hungry); prosperity (every job is holy); value (Christians value life from conception to grave). This kingdom is saturated with the knowledge of God (so Christians begin schools, universities, and branches of science; they teach literacy). It is a kingdom of justice (so Christians judge others "not by the color of their skin, but the content of their character"

[MLK] and work toward such a society). It is a kingdom that values service, even to the poor and needy (so Christians go to the streets of Calcutta [Mother Teresa]) and start microloan organizations. It is a kingdom that treats creation as sacred (so Christians work for a clean environment, stewarding creation) and respects everyone's place in it (so Christians work for property rights in underdeveloped countries). It is a kingdom of cultural beauty (so Christians work in all fields of art to the glory of God). It is a kingdom of truth and love (hence, the community of the church finds its identity as a "sign" of the kingdom).

Jesus came to bring heaven on earth. In Him we enter the kingdom of God and then live by His Spirit into its vision, both in character and work. In this, the kingdom is both *now and not yet*. We await the fullness of the kingdom in the personal return of Jesus. In that day, our efforts within the vision of the kingdom will find their fulfillment. The witness of Jesus and Scripture indicate that there is an organic unity between kingdom life now and in its fullness to come. Jesus Himself likened it to pregnancy (Mt 24:8). God's kingdom now is in the womb of this world, inseminated by the seed of Jesus (Jn 12:24, 1 Jn 3:9) and growing (Mt 24:14). There is both continuity with and difference between the child in the womb and her mother. Jesus' resurrected body itself bears witness to this organic unity. Transformed, He can bodily meet His fear-filled followers behind locked doors (Jn 20:19–20). Yet He is recognized bodily and identified by His wound marks. He is the same yet transformed, bearing witness to the kingdom's organic unity between this age and the next. This organic unity of the kingdom, the now and not yet, will be further explored in coming chapters.

Before that day of kingdom fullness, like Jesus Himself in His journey along the Christ plotline, followers of Jesus in this age must learn obedience, endure suffering, and face death—each major themes of Scripture.

CHAPTER 4

Learning Obedience

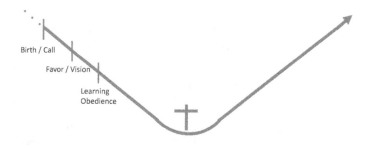

> In the days of his flesh, Jesus offered up prayers and supplications, with loud cries and tears, to him who was able to save him from death, and he was heard because of his reverence. Although he was a son, he learned obedience through what he suffered. And being made perfect, he became the source of eternal salvation to all who obey him. (Heb 5:7–9)

Jesus learned obedience. He learned obedience in His sufferings. He learned obedience in the wilderness. He learned obedience in the journey of His entire life from birth to death. And in the course of that life, His obedience grew deeper, stronger, bigger, and brighter till it reached its fullness in "obedience to the point of death, even death on a cross" (Phil 2:8).

In learning obedience, Jesus understood that the heart of obedience is love.

> A lawyer asked him (Jesus) a question to test him. "Teacher, which is the great commandment in the Law?" And he said to him, "You shall love the Lord your God with all your heart and with all your soul and with all your mind. This is the great and first commandment. And a second is like it: You shall love your neighbor as yourself. On these two commandments depend all the Law and the Prophets. (Mt 22:35–40)

Because love is the heart of the law, Jesus taught His followers to honor the laws of God (Mt 5:19), pursuing righteousness.

> You therefore must be perfect, as your heavenly Father is perfect. (Mt 5:48)

In His Sermon on the Mount, therefore, Jesus taught His followers that obedience involves not only not breaking God's will in heart, thought, and deed, it is also engaging in that will positively and creatively. For example, Jesus affirmed the Decalogue's prohibition of murder in both deed and heart.

> Everyone who is angry with his brother will be liable to judgment...and whoever says, 'You fool!' will be liable to the hell of fire. (Mt 5:22)

And then He went further in verses 23–24 to teach that obedience to the sixth command positively involves the love of forgiveness and peacemaking.

> So if you are offering your gift at the altar and there remember that your brother has something against you, leave your gift there before the altar

and go. First be reconciled to your brother and
then come and offer your gift. (Mt 5:23–24)

Jesus learned this fuller understanding of obedience because He
loved God's law. Psalm 119 is the definitive Old Testament witness
of the heart of Jesus with regard to God's law.

> Oh how I love your law! It is my meditation all
> the day... Your testimonies are wonderful; there-
> fore, my soul keeps them. The unfolding of your
> words gives light; it imparts understanding to
> the simple. I open my mouth and pant, because
> I long for your commandments. (Ps 119:97,
> 129–131)

Psalm 119 is Jesus' heart as it was His same Spirit who inspired
the writer of those words.

In the Old Covenant, the bedrock of God's law and the life of
obedience, personally and socially, is the Ten Commandments (Ex
20:1–17, Dt 5:1–21). These laws stem out of the character of God.
Hence, their introduction,

> I am the Lord your God, who brought you out
> of Egypt, out of the house of slavery. (Ex 20:2)

As such, they reveal who God is; they point to the person of
Jesus and, ultimately, in their vision of obedience, they call us to the
culture of the heavenly life that Jesus came to bring on earth. The
first commandment is

> You shall have no other gods before me.

It implies that God alone is Ultimate Reality, our Creator and
Judge. This law bears witness to Jesus as the unique "way" through
whom we come to the One and Only God (Jn 14:6). It forbids false
worship—giving allegiance to any other person, thing, or identity

above that of God Himself and an identity ground in who He is. Positively, this law calls us to the *obedience of worship*—living comprehensively in zeal for God's glory. It calls us to a life of adoration and honor to God.

The second commandment is

> You shall not make for yourself a carved image, or
> any likeness of anything that is in heaven above,
> or that is in the earth beneath, or that is in the
> water under the earth. (Ex 20:4)

This law forbids the attempt to control God through images such as shrine or talisman or superstitious belief and practice. It addresses us as humans made in the image of God and calls us to cultivate that image in our character and work. In this, it positively calls us to the *obedience of responsibility* as God's image bearers. We are not to make images of God; as His vice-regents, we are to become the image of God on earth, even as Jesus Himself was the fullness of that image incarnate (Col 1:15) in His person and work.

The third command is

> You shall not take the name of the Lord your
> God in vain.

Of course, this prohibits misusing God's name by cursing or blasphemy or even empty-headed slang—i.e., OMG. This law calls us to take the name of God with sacred seriousness. God's name is the revelation of who He is. God is not whoever we would want to make Him to be. He is who He has revealed Himself to be, in nature and Scripture and, ultimately, in Jesus, the "name above all names" (Phil 2:9). Therefore, this law calls us to the *obedience of seeking revealed truth*. We are to pursue God's truth that we might live in it. That is the life of obedience.

The fourth commandment calls us to

> remember the Sabbath day, to keep it holy.

This law forbids work one day in seven and is a call to rest on that day. In the Old Covenant, this day came at week's end. In the New Covenant secured by Jesus, this day comes at the outset of the week, for Jesus is God's rest on earth (Mt 11:28, Heb 4:3), risen on the week's first day. Through Christ, a believer labors in a week's following six days with peace and gratitude for "salvation rest" in Jesus. In its fullest understanding, this fourth law calls us to the *obedience of living in hope*, for the Sabbath day's highest calling is to renew us in the vision of eternal life through the proclamation of God's Word, the offering of prayers and praise, the enjoyment of creation, relationships, and cultural goodness.

The fifth commandment is

> Honor your father and your mother, that your
> days may be long in the land that the Lord your
> God is giving you.

It reveals God as our ultimate authority. He designates His authority in the family to the father and mother. In society, He variously designates that same authority to government, law enforcement, teachers, bosses, coaches, and church elders. This law calls us to the *obedience of submissive respect*. Further, being designated from God, all authority is subject to and accountable to God. It is authority designated for the well-being of others. In this, Jesus has been granted "all authority in heaven and on earth" (Mt 28:18) through the submission of the cross. And with the authority entrusted to Him, Jesus came "not to be served but to serve and give his life as a ransom for many" (Mk 10:45), through which His people are blessed with the well-being of heavenly life.

Jesus' explanation of the sixth commandment in His Sermon on the Mount is

> You shall not murder. (Mt 5:21–25)

It reveals God as the source of all life and calls us to the *obedience of being life-giving*. To insult others, belittle them, or "kill" them with thoughts, words, looks, and deeds is essentially to invite others to die. This command forbids such behavior. Positively, it calls us to be life-giving through our words and deeds.

> Let no corrupting talk come out of your mouths,
> but only such as is good for building up, as fits
> the occasion, that it may give grace to those who
> hear. (Eph 4:29)

To be life-giving also calls us to the obedience of forgiveness because until forgiveness is established in relationship with those who have mistreated us, that relationship is dead. Only forgiveness creates the possibility of restoration and renewal. Even so, the sixth commandment bears witness to Jesus as the One who has come to bring mankind "life" with God (Jn 11:25, 14:6).

The seventh commandment calls us to the *obedience of faithfulness.*

> You shall not commit adultery.

It bears witness to God as the One fully faithful to the promises of His Word.

> Know therefore that the Lord your God is God,
> the faithful God who keeps covenant and stead-
> fast love with those who love him and keep his
> commandments, to a thousand generations,
> and repays to their face those who hate him, by
> destroying them. He will not be slack with the
> one who hates him. He will repay him to his face.
> (Dt 7:9–10)

God is always true to His word. Therefore, this command points to Jesus as God's true covenant word among us. Certainly it forbids any unchastity in actions, talk, looks, thoughts, or desires. But more than that, it calls us to pursue faithfulness in the covenant vows of marriage as well as integrity in all our words of promise and everyday speech.

The eighth commandment is

You shall not steal.

Why? Because God is our Provider, Jehovah-Jireh (Gn 22:14), the fullness of His provision being in the person and work of Jesus. This law forbids theft. We are not to take anything that does not belong to us. We are to respect the property rights of others. Positively, it calls us to the *obedience of stewardship and generosity*, "working faithfully so that we might share with those in need" ("Heidelberg Catechism," Q and A 111).

The ninth commandment calls us to the *obedience of honesty*.

You shall not bear false witness against your neighbor.

God hates deceit in any form.

There are six things that the Lord hates, seven that are an abomination to him: haughty eyes, a lying tongue, and hands that shed innocent blood, a heart that devises wicked plans, feet that make haste to run to evil, a false witness who breathes out lies, and one who sows discord among brothers. (Prv 6:16–19)

Citing Isaiah 53:9, Peter describes Jesus as the one who

Committed no sin, neither was deceit found in his mouth. (1 Pt 2:22)

Honesty leads to a life of transparency and candidness. Such a life facilitates genuine community with others. It moves us toward the eternal community of the Triune God.

The tenth commandment bears similarity to the first. It calls us to God as our "All in All." It leads us into the *obedience of trust*, with particularity to our neighbor's belongings.

> You shall not covet your neighbor's house, wife,
> man or maidservant, ox, donkey or anything that
> belongs to your neighbor.

This command calls us to find our deepest joy in God and not in comparison to our neighbor. It is the command that revealed to the apostle Paul the depths of sin within his own heart (Rom 7:8). Could it be that his zeal for God prior to meeting Christ Jesus was charged by covetousness? This law calls us truly to rest in God and find our deepest joy in obedience for the delight of goodness itself. The first and tenth commandments bookend all obedience and bear witness to Jesus as the truly Obedient One.

That obedience of Jesus culminated in the cross. Even as His obedience grew through life, its fullest expression was evidenced at His death. There the law was fulfilled absolutely in each of the callings of the Ten Commandments—as an act of worship; as a human bearing responsibility in the image of God for the sin of the world; as a witness to truth; as one living in hope; in the honor of submission; to the end of becoming life-giving; in covenant faithfulness and perseverance; from which poured the provision of grace, God's generosity; in the honesty of love for community's sake; always and fully trusting.

> Father, into your hands I commit my spirit.
> (Luke 23:46)

If the heart of obedience is love which

> does not rejoice in wrong doing, but rejoices
> with the truth...bears all things, believes all
> things, hopes all things, endures all things (1 Cor
> 13:6–7),

then the cross of Jesus can be recognized as history's greatest act of love for God and man. Truly, in His death, Jesus became the fully obedient human.

Obedience For and In

This obedience of the *second Adam* stands juxtaposed with the disobedience of the first Adam. The calling to learn the obedience of love goes back to the garden of Eden when God entered a "covenant of works" with Adam and Eve. Obedience brings divine blessing, and had they remained obedient to God's law, they would have transitioned from a state of unconfirmed to confirmed righteousness, with a translation of their physical selves likely into that exalted state. However, in their disobedience, they were cut off from the tree of life (Gn 3:22), and sinister death entered existence for their race. Disobedience brings divine curse.

> For you are dust and to dust you shall return.
> (Gn 3:19)

Thereafter in Scripture, the obedience of Jesus stands juxtaposed with Adam's line of fallen mankind (Gn 6:5). Even among those chosen of God in His purposes of salvation—Noah (Gn 6:20–23); Abraham (Gn 16:2); Jacob (Gn 27:24); Moses (Ex 2:12); David (2 Sm 11:4)—each of their stories include disobedience to God's laws. So, too, with the nation Israel. Their disobedience to God's laws (1 Cor 10:1–10) is highlighted throughout the Old Covenant.

Jesus' obedience then becomes an obedience both *for* and *in* His people.

> For as by the one man's disobedience the many
> were made sinners, so by the one man's obedience
> the many will be made righteous. (Rom 5:19)

Through His obedience, Jesus expressed both the fullness of love for God and for those He came to save!

> For our sake he (God) made him to be sin who knew no sin, so that in him we might become the righteousness of God. (2 Cor 5:21)

In His death on the cross, Jesus satisfied the human requirements of God's law so that, through faith in Him, God's people would move from the status of curse to blessing. As a substitutionary sacrifice, He bore the curse of sin—death in its most sinister fashion, even unto God-forsakenness (Mt 27:46). Galatians 3:13–14 explains,

> Christ redeemed us from the curse of the law by becoming a curse for us, for it is written: "Cursed is everyone who is hung on a tree." He redeemed us in order that the blessing given to Abraham might come through Christ Jesus, so that by faith we might receive the promise of the Spirit. (Gal 3:13–14 NIV)

That promise of the Spirit is the anointing of the obedient heart of Jesus *in* us. In the Old Covenant, the prophet Ezekiel foretold this blessing of salvation. A day is coming, the Messianic Day, he declared, a day when God will do this work within His people:

> I will sprinkle clean water on you, and you will be clean; I will cleanse you from all your impurities and from all your idols. I will give you a new heart and put a new spirit in you; I will remove from you your heart of stone and give you a heart of flesh. And I will put my Spirit in you and move you to follow my decrees and be careful to keep my laws. (Ez 36:25–27 NIV)

In Jesus, that day has now come. Anointed with His obedient heart, a Christian comes to love God's law (Ps 119), even as Jesus loved God's law. A Christian learns to understand God's law and apply it increasingly and more meaningfully into his life of sanctification. A Spirit-born Christian appreciates the goodness of God's law.

> Now we know that the law is good, if one uses it lawfully. (1 Tm 1:8)

Proper use of God's law is to use it to know God, to relish the heart of Christ, to understand the ways of love, to be convicted of shortcomings in one's character and behavior, bringing those to God in sorrow and turning. Proper use of God's law is to never use it in the cause of self-righteous pride (Phil 3:7–8) or in comparison with others (Luke 18:11). Proper use of God's law becomes a Christian's joy because it is spiritual fellowship with Jesus.

> For this is the love of God, that we keep his commandments. And his commandments are not burdensome. For everyone who has been born of God overcomes the world. (1 Jn 5:3–4)

This is not to say that a Christian's journey along the Christ plotline of learning obedience will be easy. In Romans 7, the apostle Paul details the struggle that obedience can take as long as we yet live with our sin-stained nature. In verses 14–24, Paul makes clear that his deepest self, his truest self, his Spirit-anointed self loves and wants to do God's law. Yet that new self in Jesus lives in his "flesh" (sinful nature).

> I do not understand what I do. For what I want to do (the law) I do not do, but what I hate I do. And if I do what I do not want to do, I agree that the law is good. As it is, it is no longer I myself who do it, but it is sin living in me... What a wretched man I am! Who will rescue me from

this body of death? Thanks be to God—through Jesus Christ our Lord! (Rom 7:15–17, 24–25 NIV)

Indeed, thanks be to God, one day we will be free from the struggle to learn obedience. In that day, obedience will come as naturally as breathing. That freedom from struggle will come in our future glorification. But till that day, what motivates us to continue to learn obedience in Jesus?

Obedience Motivations

Chief among motives is the goodness of God who, in love and grace, has authored our salvation! Thus, a Christian pursues obedience in thanks, joy, freedom, and praise to the glory of God.

We love because He first loved us. (1 Jn 4:19)

Beyond this primary motivation, there are at least three other good reasons, ones which fix our eyes on the Christ plotline and our future in Him.

Obedience brings blessing; disobedience, curse. This was clear in the original Adamic covenant (Gn 2:16–17) and every subsequent covenant that God entered with His people. In the unfolding of salvation, covenants are not abolished; they are fulfilled. The dynamics of their realities continue into the fullness of God's covenantal life in Christ Jesus (Mt 5:17). The goodness of that covenant is that Jesus leads us into the promised blessings of obedience that Moses bore witness to in Deuteronomy 28:1–14. In obedience,

The Lord will establish you as people holy to himself... And the Lord will make you abound in prosperity, in the fruit of your womb and in the fruit of your livestock and in the fruit of your ground, within the land that the Lord swore to your fathers to give you. (Dt 28:9, 11)

This "health and wealth" of obedience, however, must be understood in the context of God's kingdom on earth. Measures of it materially may come to us in this sin-stained, broken age of the earth, but not necessarily. Suffering, hardship, and loss come to every believer in this age (see chapters ahead). That said, "kingdom health and wealth" through obedience certainly does begin to come to a Christian even now in the "fruit of the Spirit"—love, joy, peace, patience, kindness, goodness, faithfulness, gentleness, and self-control (Gal 5:22–23). But it is in the future age of God's kingdom on earth, the age all believers live toward, the "new heavens and earth" (Rv 21–22), that the fullness of obedience blessings are realized to those in Christ. Christians learn obedience toward that vision of blessing. In that vision,

> blessed is the man who does not walk in the counsel of the wicked or stand in the way of sinners or sit in the seat of mockers. But his delight is in the law of the Lord, and on that law he meditates day and night—becoming like a tree planted by streams of water, which yields its fruit in season and whose leaf does not wither. Whatever he does prospers. Not so the wicked! They are like chaff that the wind blows away. (Ps 1:1–4 NIV)

Another motive for a Christian to learn obedience is tied to this relationship of fulfillment that the future age has with our present age. The life of obedience is living into the character of God, the culture of heaven, and a Christian's future self. As the Ten Commandments make clear, the law of God reflects *who He is*—Ultimate Reality. Each person must prepare to encounter God's character. Learning obedience prepares us for Judgment Day. But more than that, for those who have begun the journey of repentance and trust in God's love in Christ, learning obedience equips us for heavenly life. It cultivates lungs which can deeply breathe in the atmosphere of heaven on earth. Obedience now will know its reward then. In Christ, therefore, a vision of a believer's future self calls forth obedience—a vision of trust, worship, rest, faithfulness, honesty, generosity, courage, submission, worship. That vision leads a person into repentance and trust in Jesus and then the journey of obedient fellowship with the life of His Spirit. A power to shun disobedience, therefore, is in naming it as a false identity. Correlated, learning obedience is growing into a Christian's future self. Therein is power to resist temptation and pursue obedience with hope and joy!

Connected to this vision of the Christian's future life is the life of service promised in the new heaven and earth. In that age, Jesus promised that our life of obedience now will know its reward in leadership then. In His parable of the ten minas (a mina equals three months' wages) in Luke 19:11–27, Jesus indicated that those who were productive with the kingdom measure granted to them in this age will be rewarded in the age to come.

> You shall have authority over ten cities. (Luke 19:17)

A similar parable in Matthew 25 ends up stating heavenly reward as

> I will set you over much. (Mt 25:21)

The Apostle Paul too, in his vision of life in the next age, describes believers as being granted the wisdom to serve the world and angels in judgment (1 Cor 6:1–3). Jesus' own life of learning obedience in this age was essential for His ministry in His glorified state. He has become our "Great High Priest" (Heb 4:14–5:10) because He faced temptation as we do, yet remained sinless, so

> we approach his throne of grace with confidence
> so that we may receive mercy and find grace to
> help us in our time of need. (Heb 4:16 NIV)

Jesus' obedience in this age created a context for His service in the age to come. As His "kingdom of priests" (Rv 1:6), our life of obedience now will also find its particular meaning of service in the age to come.

From Genesis to Revelation, all of Scripture is colored by the theme of obedience. Praise God that that theme ultimately draws us to Jesus as the Obedient Servant of God. Through Him, a believer journeys along the calling of obedience, even as Jesus Himself did. That journey is begun on the foundation of forgiveness—Christ's obedience for us. It continues in the power of the Spirit—Christ's obedience in us. That journey becomes most intense in the context of suffering.

CHAPTER 5

Suffering

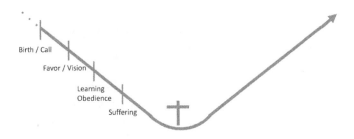

Birth / Call

Favor / Vision

Learning
Obedience

Suffering

On the night He was betrayed, Jesus, through His knowledge of Scripture, was mindful of His impending suffering. His thoughts were with King David whose life story He was about to fulfill. During the Passover meal that He shared with His disciples in the upper room, Jesus quotes David's words from Psalm 41:9,

> He who shares my bread has lifted up his heel
> against me. (Jn 13:18 NIV, also Mt 26:23–24)

Jesus is referring to His disciple Judas who is about to betray Him with a kiss.

In its original context, Psalm 41:9 is likely a reference to David's trusted counselor Ahithophel whose "advice was like that of one who inquires of God" (2 Sm 16:23). Ahithophel had "raised his heel" against

David in the time when David's own son, Absalom, had conspired to overthrow his father as king. In gathering forces to commit this insurrection, Ahithophel chose to join Absalom's movement. His was a key addition. With Ahithophel's betrayal in place, David was forced to flee his rightful throne in Jerusalem. His departure was an exile, a type of "death"—especially as David's flight takes him across the River Jordan which, in Scripture, regularly symbolizes death. David's exile beyond the Jordan is exactly what Jesus knows is about to happen to Himself, a pending death triggered by the betrayal of a close disciple.

Some of the key events of this story in David's life (2 Sm 14–20) are worth noting as they bear witness to King Jesus. David's suffering and "death" are at the immediate hand of his own family (Absalom) as Jesus' were.

> He came to his own, and his own people did not
> receive him. (Jn 1:11)

David's flight beyond the Jordan divides people—some remain loyal to him, others don't, i.e., Shimei (2 Sm 15:5–8), he of the "household of Saul" (unregenerate man). David voluntarily enters this exile (15:14) but does so in trust before God and hopeful of a "return" (resurrection).

> Then the king said to Zadok, "Carry the ark of
> God back into the city. If I find favor in the eyes
> of the Lord, he will bring me back and let me see
> both it and his dwelling place. But if he says, I
> have no pleasure in you, behold, here I am, let
> him do to me what seems good to him." (2 Sm
> 15:25–26)

Indeed, after defeating Absalom (Satan) on the east side of the Jordan, Jesus "found favor with the Lord," just as David did, his return to Jerusalem's throne foretelling Jesus' resurrection. In that return, King David invites others to "cross over the Jordan" with him (2 Sm 19:37–40)—death is conquered in King Jesus. So those who go to meet him on the east side of the Jordan ("He who loses his life for my sake will find it") cross over with David to join in his reign. And what of Ahithophel? His plight foretells Judas'. After Absalom chooses to reject his advice (17:14), Ahithophel realizes that his decision to side with Absalom was in error, and he hung himself (17:23, cf. Mt 27:3–5).

As in David's story, the suffering of the anointed of God at the hands of the ungodly is a theme throughout Scripture. Each instance of this type of suffering finds its ultimate meaning in Jesus' sufferings as the Anointed One. At the beginning of the Bible, when jealous Cain murders his innocent brother, Abel, the Lord declares,

> The voice of your brother's blood is crying to me
> from the ground. (Gn 4:10)

All mankind is implicated in the spilled blood of our brother Jesus. It declares our universal guilt. Again at the end of the Bible (Rv 6:9–10), those souls "who had been slain because of the word of God and the testimony they had maintained call out in a loud voice,"

> O Sovereign Lord, holy and true, how long
> before you will judge and avenge our blood on
> those who dwell on the earth? (Rv 6:10)

The anointed suffer on account of the ungodly.

Between these two texts, this type of suffering is also seen in the Esau and Jacob story.

> Now Esau hated Jacob because of the blessing
> with which his father had blessed him, and Esau
> said to himself, "The days of mourning for my
> father are approaching; then I will kill my brother
> Jacob. (Gn 27:41)

Joseph's suffering at the hands of his brothers is chronicled in chapter 1 of this book. Moses suffers as he leads the people of God through the wilderness, even at the hand of his own brother and sister (Nm 12)! David suffers, not only at the hand of his own son Absalom but before that in his service to Saul. Jealous of David's popularity, Saul forces David to flee into the wilderness (1 Sm 19–30). In that context, David writes many psalms lamenting his suffering:

> I say to God my Rock, "Why have you forgotten me? Why must I go about mourning, oppressed by the enemy?" My bones suffer mortal agony as my foes taunt me, saying to me all day long, "Where is your God?" (Ps 42:9–10)

See also Psalm 3, 22, 57–59, 73, 102—each bear witness to suffering in the Christ life. The prophets, too, testify to this type of suffering. Jeremiah is chief among them. He was mocked and ridiculed (Jer 20:7) by the ungodly, put in stocks (20:2) and chained (40:1), even put in a pit and left to die, though rescued (38:6–15).

In the New Testament, the apostle Paul describes this type of suffering as "sharing in the sufferings of Christ" (Phil 3:10) through which, as promised in the Christ plotline, believers "attain to the resurrection from the dead" (3:11). Elsewhere, Paul makes plain,

> Indeed, all who desire to live a godly life in Christ Jesus will be persecuted. (2 Tm 3:12)

And in His beatitudes, Jesus names the blessedness in this type of suffering:

> Blessed are those persecuted because of righteousness, for theirs is the kingdom of heaven. Blessed are you when people insult you, persecute you and falsely say all kinds of evil against you because of me. Rejoice and be glad, because great is your reward in heaven, for in the same way they persecuted the prophets who were before you. (Mt 5:10–12 NIV)

The greatest blessing in suffering for the sake of God's righteousness is fellowship with Jesus, the "man of sorrow, acquainted with grief" (Is 53:3). This type of suffering then becomes witness to Jesus and a form of ministry (see Paul in Acts 16:16-40 versus Acts 22:29 regarding his rights as a Roman citizen). In this, Jesus is the fulfillment of Scripture's journey of suffering.

Punitive Suffering

Another type of suffering in Scripture is punitive. When Adam and Eve disobey God, there are consequences. They are judged. Their life is cursed (Gn 3:14–19) with pain in childbirth, disruption in relationship, sweat in the toil of work, and ultimately, in the disintegration of death—"dust you are and to dust you shall return." Disobedience brings curse as punishment. This type of suffering, too, bears witness to Jesus' life and its meaning. In His sufferings, He bore the curse of sin (Gal 3:13). Through His pain, a new humanity was born; in the disruption of relationship with His heavenly Father—

> My God, my God, why have you forsaken me?
> (Mt 27:46)

—a sure covenant of love was established with God for His people; by the sweat and toil of His prayer in Gethsemane, He remained the obedient, sinless sacrifice for us; and by His cursed death we are granted eternal life.

The Exodus event also bears witness to Jesus' sufferings. Through acts of judgment against Pharaoh and the Egyptians, God brings deliverance to His people. Those acts begin with Aaron's rod turning into a snake (a visual of Christ on the cross) and Egypt's water turning to blood (Ex 7). The plagues end with total darkness over the land (cf. Mt 27:45) and the death of the firstborn son (Ex 10–11). These acts of judgment bring freedom to God's people, releasing them to begin a journey through the wilderness to the promised land.

On that journey, God's people suffer when they disobey. Facing the giants in Canaan, they cower in unbelief (Nm 14). As a result, that generation of Israelites is cut off from life in the promised land as Jesus was "cut off from the land of the living" (Is 53:8). Later they complain about conditions in the wilderness, and venomous snakes are sent among them (Nm 21). Only by looking at the pole-raised bronze snake are they healed.

> And as Moses lifted up the serpent in the wilderness, so must the Son of Man be lifted up, that whoever believes in him may have eternal life. (Jn 3:14)

> But he was pierced for our transgressions; he was crushed for our iniquities; upon him was the chastisement that brought us peace, and with his wounds we are healed. (Is 53:5)

The Firstborn Son whose heel was struck by the Serpent (Gn 3:15) was lifted up in the wilderness of this age so that He might crush that Serpent's head. Looking at and trusting His sufferings, we are healed and have true life.

Discipline

Because Jesus fully atoned for the curse of sin, His people are free from condemnation before God (Rom 8:1). In Christ, we begin a life within God's favor. In that life, suffering is then understood in the context of sanctification and discipline.

> Endure hardship as discipline; God is treating you as sons. For what son is not disciplined by his father?... Our fathers disciplined us for a little while as they thought best; but God disciplines us for our good, that we may share in his holiness. (Heb 12:7, 10 NIV)

70

As in Jesus' journey, God has good purposes in our sufferings (Rom 8:28). In Jesus' life, they deepened Him in obedience (Heb 5:8) and led to the redemption of His people from the curse of sin. Once redeemed in Christ, God uses sufferings to sanctify His people. Through suffering, we cultivate perseverance and maturity (Jas 1:2–4). Through suffering, God leads us into humility and dependence, as with Paul's "thorn in the flesh."

> My grace is sufficient for you, for my power is made perfect in weakness. (2 Cor 12:9)

Through suffering, God deepens us in His comfort and grows in us compassion for others (2 Cor 1:3–4). He also works in us longings for the fullness of heavenly life (Phil 1:23). Through suffering, the Spirit softens our hearts to be convicted by sin (Ps 32) that we might confess it and grow in righteousness.

> Search me, O God, and know my heart! Try me and know my thoughts! And see if there be any grievous way in me, and lead me in the way everlasting! (Ps 139:23–24)

The essence of wisdom is to mature through suffering. This is a key theme in the book of Proverbs, one that differentiates the wise from the fool.

> He who heeds discipline shows the way to life, but whoever ignores correction leads others astray. (Prv 10:17 NIV)

> Whoever loves discipline loves knowledge, but he who hates reproof is stupid. (Prv 12:1)

> A wise son hears his father's instruction, but a scoffer does not listen to rebuke. (Prv 13:1)

He who ignores discipline despises himself, but whoever heeds correction gains understanding. The fear of the Lord teaches a man wisdom, and humility comes before honor. (Prv 15:32–33 NIV)

As the wisdom of God on earth, Jesus fulfills these proverbs. They bear witness to His life and His Spirit in us. As Paul writes,

Christ Jesus has become for us wisdom from God—that is, our righteousness, holiness and redemption. (1 Cor 1:30 NIV)

Lament in Christ

The book of Job makes clear that not all suffering is punitive or disciplinary. Job is "blameless and upright, a man who fears God and shuns evil" (Jb 1:8). Yet Satan is permitted to bring suffering into his life to test his faith.

"Does Job fear God for nothing?" asserts Satan... "Stretch out your hand and strike everything he has, and he will surely curse you to your face." (Jb 1:9, 11 NIV)

So God allows Job to be tested with pain and loss of property, family, and health. In response, Job laments in sorrow, anger, confusion, despair, complaint. He laments his life. He laments the loss of meaning that suffering brings. He laments the absence of God's presence. He laments the seeming injustice of life.

If only my anguish could be weighed and all my misery be placed on the scales! It would surely outweigh the sand of the seas—no wonder my words have been impetuous. The arrows of the

Almighty are in me, my spirit drinks in their poi-
son. (Jb 6:2–4 NIV)

The Scriptures affirm this response to suffering. To lament is
to become honest with the evil and wrong in God's good creation.
Up to 65 of the 150 psalms can be classified as songs of lament, the
largest category of psalms. They are songs of complaints, anxiety,
protest, distress.

How long, O Lord? Will you forget me forever?
How long will you hide your face from me? How
long must I wrestle with my thoughts and every
day have sorrow in my heart? How long will my
enemy triumph over me? (Ps 13:1–2 NIV)

These lament psalms typically end on a note of trust, and in
that, they bring understanding of the heart of Jesus as He wrestled
honestly with the mistreatment, evil, and suffering impacting His
life. On the cross, He, like Job, like David, wondered, *Will you forget
me forever?*

My God, my God, why have you forsaken me?

Yet He died in trust, expecting God to vindicate His life.

Father, into your hands I commit my spirit!
(Luke 23:46)

The Scriptures call us to lament the loss of things good and
holy. This, too, finds meaning in our response to Christ crucified.
When King Saul and his son Jonathon lose their lives on Mount
Gilboa (1 Sm 31), David mourns, weeps, and fasts—even though
Saul had been seeking to kill David. The anointed king had died—it
calls for grief. An Amalekite who reported Saul's death, even claiming
ownership for its execution (2 Sm 1), is slain by David because he
failed to weep over the death of the Lord's anointed. Likewise, the

Bible book titled Lamentations is an extended poem mourning the destruction of Jerusalem. God's holy city and its temple have been decimated by the forces of proud Babylon—name it, grieve it. The event foretells the suffering and destruction of God's holy Son, Jesus.

> How the Lord has covered the Daughter of Zion with the cloud of his anger! He has hurled down the splendor of Israel from heaven to earth; he has not remembered his footstool in the day of his anger. (Lam 2:1 NIV)

When we lament aright, it gives opportunity to repent of the sin which contributed to Jesus' sufferings. The Apostle Paul distinguished between godly and worldly lament in 2 Corinthians 7. He commends the Corinthians,

> for you became sorrowful as God intended... Godly sorrow brings repentance that leads to salvation and leaves no regret, but worldly sorrow brings death. See what this godly sorrow has produced in you: what earnestness, what eagerness to clear yourselves, what indignation, what alarm, what longing, what concern, what readiness to see justice done. (2 Cor 7:9–11 NIV)

Even so, a Christian learns to lament sin and suffering and loss in the context of Jesus' crucifixion, appreciating that His sufferings lead into the godly repentance of salvation.

One reason for the Bible's enduring popularity is its honesty about life. Life is difficult, often confusing, painful, and sorrowful. Suffering is a key theme throughout the pages of the Bible. Reading these passages in Christ draws us into the sufferings of the Messiah for the sake of creation's salvation. In Jesus' sufferings, there is a message of redemption and hope beyond loss and pain. That hope comes on the other side of death itself.

CHAPTER 6

Death

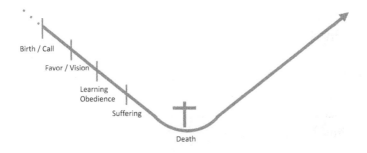

Birth / Call

Favor / Vision

Learning
Obedience

Suffering

Death

Weeping may tarry for the night, but joy comes with the morning.
—Psalm 30:5

We come now to the central pulse in all Scripture—death and resurrection. The movement "through death to new life" is key to understanding the Bible, even as it is fulfilled in the person of Jesus. In terms of our Christ plotline, death and resurrection is the climax event of its story, a climax graphed not as apex but as the bottom of the valley, a nadir. The result of this climactic event completely changes the ongoing life of Jesus and any person in Christ.

(Note: Though graphed inversely, the cross truly is a "high point" in the Christ plotline in that it most fully reveals the self-giving love of God in Jesus, the humility and servant-heartedness of God in Jesus, and the victory of God in Jesus over sin and evil. Hence, in this descent of Jesus, we are invited to "comprehend with all the saints what is the breadth and length and height and depth, and to know the love of Christ that surpasses knowledge, that you may be filled with all the fullness of God" [Eph 3:18–19]).

Jesus Himself predicted His sufferings, death, and resurrection. After His disciples correctly identify Jesus as the Christ,

> He then began to teach them that the Son of Man must suffer many things and be rejected by the elders, chief priests and teachers of the law, and that he must be killed and after three days rise again. He spoke plainly about this. (Mk 8:31–32 NIV, cf. also Mt 17:22, Luke 9:22, Jn 12:24)

What led Jesus to know this? Undoubtedly, His knowledge of Scripture was a chief reason. Isaiah 52:13–53:12 foretells a Messiah who will be "pierced for our transgressions, crushed for our iniquities." Yet after the suffering of his soul, "he will see the light of life and be satisfied" (Is 53:11). The psalms, too, speak of the suffering, death, and blessed future of the Messiah.

> But you, O Lord, do not be far off! O you my help, come quickly to my aid! Deliver my soul from the sword, my precious life from the power of the dog! Save me from the mouth of the lion! You have rescued me from the horns of the wild oxen! I will tell of your name to my brothers; in the midst of the congregation, I will praise you. (Ps 22:19–22)

More than these direct references to death and resurrection, the Old Testament narratives anticipate the Messiah's death and resurrection. They are to be read in Christ. It is significant that in Genesis 1, each day begins in darkness, after which the sun rises—light conquering darkness! The story of each sunrise bears witness to death and resurrection. Likewise do the seasons—after the death of winter comes the new life of spring. The Old Testament story that Jesus Himself cited as a sign of His death and resurrection was that of Jonah.

> For just as Jonah was three days and three nights in the belly of the great fish, so will the Son of man be three days and three nights in the heart of the earth. (Mt 12:40)

Reading the Jonah story in Christ helps us understand God's judgment against sin in Jesus' death (ch. 1:15) and then how to respond to it in repentance. In the belly of the fish, Jonah prays,

> Those who pay regard to vain idols forsake their hope of steadfast love. But I with a voice of thanksgiving will sacrifice to you; what I have vowed I will pay. Salvation belongs to the Lord! (Jon 2:8–9)

Other Old Testament stories of descent and ascent, confinement and release, exile and return, destruction and rebuilding, separation and reunion foretell Jesus' death and resurrection. Reading each of them in Christ sheds insight on the meaning of Jesus' death and resurrection.

In the lives of individuals, Daniel is confined in the lion's den and then delivered (Dn 6), thwarting the schemes of his enemies. Read in Christ, the Daniel story helps us appreciate how the schemes of Jesus' enemies—the religious establishment and the forces of evil—were not only thwarted by His death and resurrection, Daniel's deliverance leads to his exaltation!

Joseph is unjustly confined in prison, then released and exalted (Gn 41)—the messianic King exalted to the right hand of the Almighty; Adam descends into his deep sleep of death (from which his bride is taken), then awakens (Gn 2). Through His death, Jesus is given His bride, the church, who is "bone of my bones and flesh of my flesh, the two becoming one, a relationship in which there is no shame" (Gn 2:23–25).

Jacob is exiled from the promised land (to Padan Aram) and returns (Gn 28–32). He, too, gains his bride through that exile. Noah is exiled from his land (into the ark) and returns (Gn 6, 9), the progenitor of a new humanity; David descends into the valley to take on Goliath and ascends triumphantly (1 Sm 17)—the head of Satan chopped off in the triumph of Jesus' crucifixion. Later in life, he abandons his throne, descends to and crosses the Jordan River—territory in which he defeats the usurper, Absalom—and then returns, crossing the Jordan again, ascending to Jerusalem's throne. Each of the citizens of David's land must make a decision in that descent— do they join him or not? Likewise, Jesus' descent is a dividing event revealing spiritual loyalties. Moses descends from Sinai with the Law in hand. Confronted by the idolatry of God's people, the Law (Jesus being the Law embodied) is "broken to pieces" (Ex 32:19), only to be restored again (Ex 34:1–2). Even Elijah's story of leaving the promised land (on account of Israel's wickedness), going to Sidon—where he raises a widow's son before returning—bears witness to the messianic movements of death and resurrection. The Word of God goes and comes back in Jesus' death and resurrection.

On the national scale, Israel, too, features stories of death and resurrection. Their exodus from Egyptian slavery, passing through the Red Sea (symbol of death), is one such example. In every Christian baptism, we are led by our second Moses, Jesus, who brings us out of slavery to sin and leads us through the waters of death (Rom 6:1–4) on to the journey toward the promised land. After their wilderness wanderings, Israel, too, must pass through the Jordan River to enter the promised land (Jo 3). This death speaks also of the physical death of someone in Christ, prior to receiving his spiritual inheritance.

Later in national life, the capture of the ark of the covenant by the godless Philistines foretells Jesus descent into the hands of the enemies. But then the ark returns—and later is exalted in Zion. Read in Christ, the story of the ark's journey witnesses to the miraculous power that raised Jesus from the dead (1 Sm 6:7–9)—what mother walks away from her newborn offspring? Prior to the ark's exaltation to Jerusalem, there is a death that occurs. Innocent Uzzah dies on account of David's and the priesthood's neglect (2 Sm 6). But once that sign of the presence of God is established in the city of David, God personally promises to David that

> I will raise up your offspring after you, who shall come from your body, and I will establish his kingdom. He shall build a house for my name, and I will establish the throne of his kingdom forever. (2 Sm 7:12–13)

That is God's promise fulfilled in Christ.

Related to this, the destruction of the temple by Babylon (2 Chr 36) foreshadows the destruction of the presence of God in the person of Jesus, both deaths being acts of God's judgment against sin. But that was not the end of the temple's story—it was raised again (Ezr 6)! The same is true of the holy city of Jerusalem—destroyed and rebuilt (2 Chr. 36, Neh 1–2).

These Old Testament narratives certainly shaped Jesus' understanding of His messianic journey. But so, too, did meta-narratives within His own life. Early in life, Jesus escapes to Egypt on account of Herod's jealousy, and then, as true Israel, He is called "out of Egypt" (Mt 2:15). At His baptism (Mt 3), Jesus descends in humility and service below the Jordan waters, then ascends, hearing God's word of affirmation. "This is my beloved son with whom I am well pleased." He further descends in obedience into the wilderness, conquering evil, and returns "in the power of the Spirit" (Luke 4:14). Feeding the multitude, Jesus breaks bread (a foreshadow of His coming death), through which five thousand are fed—the miracle being a sign of the global feeding of His resurrection life. On the Mount of Transfiguration, Jesus fellowships with Moses and Elijah. They tell Him of His impending death, and then coming down from that mountain, Jesus meets a demonized boy (Mk 9). Prior to exorcising that evil spirit, the boy falls "dead" (v. 27) on account of an attack. But Jesus "takes him by the hand and lifts him to his feet and he stood up" (v. 28). Death and resurrection confirmed. Jesus understood this destiny, not only from His knowledge of the Old Testament but from those anticipatory events in His personal life. Immediately after the events of this boy's deliverance, Jesus takes His disciples into Galilee and says to them,

> The Son of Man is going to be delivered into the hands of men, and they will kill him. And when he is killed, after three days he will rise. (Mk 9:31)

Death's Many Meanings

What is death then to a person in Christ? (The following chapter will focus on resurrection in Christ.) Because of Jesus' death and resurrection, death takes on multiple meanings in Christ.

First off, death is recognized as an *enemy* (1 Cor 15:26). It is an intruder in God's good creation. It is a consequence of sin (Rom 6:23). Death, as mankind experiences it—we who are all genealogical descendants of Adam—entered creation upon Adam's disobedience (Gn 2:17, 3:19). We can only speculate about the nature of Adam's physical self prior to the *fall* into sin. During that period of probation, Adam was without sin and may have had a physical nature awaiting a "glory-translation" (1 Cor 15:43) upon the fulfillment of his term of obedience. If his story is read in Christ, it may have been that his original physical self was no different than pre-Adamic "mankind," though his spiritual self was unique in having had God "breathe into his nostrils the breath of life and become a living being" (Gn 2:7). This condition as a "living being" was nourished by the Tree of Life (Gn 2:22) in the garden of Eden, the *tree* being a type of Christ Jesus (Rv 22:2).

Upon disobedience, however, Adam and Eve were banished from the garden, lest they attempt to fellowship with the Tree of Life in their sin-stained condition. This leads to a deeper understanding of death as *separation*. Sin separates us from God, the impure from the pure, the unholy from the holy (Is 59:2). The result of this is death, God being the "life" of all things. "The wages of sin is death"

(Rom 6:23). Upon our fall into sin in Adam, mankind immediately became spiritually dead. "In Adam, all die" (1 Cor 15:22).

> And you were dead in the trespasses and sins in which you once walked, following the course of this world, following the prince of the power of the air. (Eph 2:1–2)

Our physical death, therefore, now is a sign of this spiritual condition, our separation from God. We are each born dead in sin.

Despite sin bringing immediate spiritual death, our physical deaths are not immediate on account of God's plan of salvation. In declaring the cursed results of sin (Gn 3:14–19), God also "clothed mankind in garments of skin" (v. 21) in order to begin a plan of salvation—"an offspring of the woman who will crush the head of the serpent, even while having his heel struck" (v. 15). Therefore, while our physical death is a sign of our spiritual separation from God, it is also a *message and a warning*. As a message, death is a call to learn of God's plan of salvation and return to Him (Acts 3:19–20). As a warning, physical death is also a sign of eternal death. Revelation 20 describes this eternal death as the "second death." We are yet today in the "Day of Salvation" (2 Cor 6:2). But there will come a time when this salvation day ends, and Judgment Day comes. It is a day when

> the sea gives up the dead that are in it and death and Hades give up the dead that are in it, and each person is judged according to what he has done. Then death and Hades will be thrown into the lake of fire. The lake of fire is the second death. If anyone's name was not found written in the book of life, he is thrown into the lake of fire. (Rv 20:13–15 NIV)

Every physical death is a warning of this second, eternal death.

This warning leads us into the meaning of Jesus' unique death. Through Jesus' death, God has initiated His plan of salvation for mankind and all creation. Jesus' death was physical and spiritual. He bore the punishment of separation from God (Mt 27:46). In this, He justly atoned for the sins of all who repent and put their trust in His sacrifice for sin (Rom 3:25). He is God's gift of love for the world (Jn 3:16) so that all might return to Him and not perish in eternal death. Each human death then is an *invitation* to know the meaning of Jesus' unique human death, a meaning authenticated by God in Jesus' resurrection from the dead.

> For our sake he (God) made him (Jesus) to be sin who knew no sin, so that in him we might become the righteousness of God. (2 Cor 5:21)

Through Jesus' death, we are invited to be reconciled to God and begin eternal life today. Jesus declared,

> Truly, truly, I say to you, whoever hears my word and believes him who sent me has eternal life. He does not come into judgment but has passed from death to life. (Jn 5:24)

In Jesus, eternal life is not something awaiting a believer upon physical death. Eternal life is spiritual fellowship with God in Christ begun today! This leads to yet another understanding of death as a *calling*. When Jesus calls someone to be His follower, He invites that person to "die."

> And whoever does not take his cross and follow me is not worthy of me. Whoever finds his life will lose it, and whoever loses his life for my sake will find it. (Mt 10:38–39)

To begin eternal life, we give up our life for the sake of Jesus' honor and obedience. This is salvation. This is life in Christ. Our spiritual death is at the root of it, a part of our new *identity* in Christ. The apostle Paul describes it this way:

> I have been crucified with Christ. It is no longer I who live, but Christ who lives in me. And the

life I now live in the flesh I live by faith in the
Son of God, who loved me and gave himself for
me. (Gal 2:20)

In Christ, the "old self" is dead (Rom 6:6). This refers to our
former identity as one who is yet dead to God, living only according
to the dictates of sinful nature, the world, Satan, "the ruler of the
kingdom of the air." In salvation, that self is dead in Christ! A new
self, an eternal self, a "Christ self" has begun.

If anyone is in Christ, he is a new creation. The
old has passed away; behold, the new has come.
(2 Cor 5:17)

Not that the old self does not continue to bear sway on our
lives. As long as we live in these mortal physical bodies, that old self
with its sin nature will yet bear its influence upon our lives. Yet it is
not fundamentally who a Christian is! Our identity is in Christ. The
old self is crucified, and so we "count ourselves dead to sin but alive
to God in Christ Jesus" (Rom 6:11). In this sense, each choice of
obedience is a death to self so that the life of Christ may be manifest
in us.

Which brings us to one final meaning of death. Death is a *passage* to greater life. This is true of spiritual death. As Jesus promised,
"he who loses his life for my sake will find it...one hundred-fold"
(Mt 19:29)! It is also true of physical death. Jesus incorporates both
these promises in His great claim,

I am the resurrection and the life. Whoever
believes in me, though he die, yet shall he live,
and everyone who lives and believes in me shall
never die. (Jn 11:25–26)

Physical death for the believer is a birth canal into greater life in
Jesus. "To be away from the body is to be at home with the Lord" (2

Cor 5:8) To be sure, the salvation longing of the body is for the great Day of Resurrection when

> that which is sown perishable is raised imperishable; sown in dishonor, is raised in glory; sown in weakness, is raised in power; sown a natural body, raised a spiritual body. (1 Cor 15:42–44 NIV)

That day will begin *life after life after death*. That day will come in conjunction with our Lord Jesus' triumphant return and the Judgment Day. Until then, when a believer dies, he is promised to be present with the Lord in safety and rest.

> And I heard a voice from heaven saying, "Write this: Blessed are the dead who die in the Lord from now on." "Blessed indeed," says the Spirit, "that they may rest from their labors, for their deeds follow them!" (Rv 14:13)

Sleep is the dominant New Testament image for those dead in Christ who are awaiting the Resurrection Day.

> For since we believe that Jesus died and rose again, even so, through Jesus, God will bring with him those who have fallen asleep. (1 Thes 4:14)

Jesus Himself understood physical death in this way (cf. Jn 11:11, Mt 9:24). Along with rest and safety, it, too, appears from the book of Revelation that the dead in Christ are engaged in praise (ch. 5:9–17) and intercession.

> How long, Sovereign Lord, holy and true, until you judge the inhabitants of the earth and avenge our blood? (6:10 NIV)

And some, like Moses and Elijah on the Mount of Transfiguration with Jesus (Mk 9:2–13), might be granted "special assignment" in God's kingdom purposes. In this, the dead Samuel's coming to Saul is rather humorous. Like a bear prematurely coming out of hibernation, he asks, "Why have you disturbed me by bringing me up?" (1 Sm 28:15). What's worse than being pulled out of a wonderful rest? As the apostle puts it, to depart and be with Christ is "better by far" (Phil 1:23). Such beginnings of glory await a believer who dies in Christ, yet they are only beginnings. The full measure of glory awaits the return of King Jesus to consummate this age of the earth, bring judgment, and translate our lives into the fullness of His current glory—the Resurrection Day!

CHAPTER 7

Glorification: Resurrection

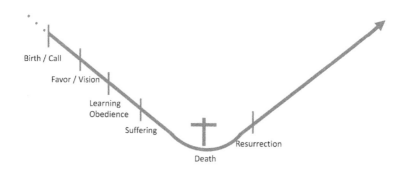

Thus says Cyrus king of Persia, "The Lord, the God of heaven, has given me all the kingdoms of the earth, and he charged me to build him a house at Jerusalem, which is in Judah. Whoever is among you of all his people, may the Lord his God be with him. Let him go up."
—2 Chronicles 36:23

Now there's an Easter text! Out of the blue, at a point in time when Israel was in exile, dispersed and far from home, when it appeared that Israel's story was at an end, when the city of Jerusalem and its holy temple had been crushed and destroyed, then comes the word of the "Almighty Ruler" King Cyrus: "Let the Temple be raised again!" Destruction and death is not the end of the messianic narrative. New life is! And that risen life is not the Messiah's alone. "Any of his people among you," join in! "Let him go up" and be part of establishing the presence of God on earth in this age. Rebuild the temple and establish Jerusalem, the society built around that presence of God to His honor and glory (cf. book of Nehemiah).

"Will you join in this company of rebuilders?" the priest Ezra wonders. In the book titled by Ezra's name, King Cyrus' proclamation also begins that writing. Thereafter (Ezr 2) comes a list of those who choose to accept the invitation. It is the veritable "Book of Life."

> If anyone's name was not found written in the book of life, he was thrown into the lake of fire. (Rv 20:15)

Chapter 3 of Ezra then records the building of the temple, a building which stood into Jesus' day, a building that underwent various refurbishments, particularly under Herod the Great. That rebuilding begins with the establishment of the altar of sacrifice, after which the foundations for the temple are laid both with rejoicing and lament, those in lament yet longing for the fullness of the glory of the temple, such being the Christian's joy and longing in this age. Chapters 4–5 of Ezra describe the opposition that the rebuilding project faces.

> Then the people of the land discouraged the people of Judah and made them afraid to build and bribed counselors against them to frustrate their purpose. (Ezr 4:4–5)

Nevertheless, the "gates of hell shall not prevail against the church that Jesus is building" (Mt 16:18). God sends prophets such as Haggai and Zechariah to inspire the rebuilding project. Ezra 6 then records the completion and dedication of the temple (vv. 13–18). Thereafter, others join the holy community in Jerusalem (ch. 7–8), although these people commit the sin of becoming intermarried with those outside the "holy race" (ch. 9:2). This sin they confess and turn from (ch. 10) in a renewal of their resurrection identity. Such understanding is reading the book of Ezra in Christ.

The resurrection narrative, however, is not only foretold in Israel's national story (from slavery to exodus, from exile to return); it, too, is seen in the personal lives of Old Testament witnesses. Here are a few samples. Jonah, whose confinement in the whale led Jesus to anticipate His confinement in the heart of the earth (Mt 12:40), was "vomited out of that fish on to dry ground" (Jn 2:19) Likewise, Joseph was brought up out of prison and Daniel out of the lions' den. Daniel's three friends—Shadrach, Meshach, and Abednego—were delivered out of King Nebuchadnezzar's fire.

> The fire had not had any power over the bodies of those men. The hair of their heads was not singed, their cloaks were not harmed, and no smell of fire had come upon them. (Dn 3:27)

Gideon was a great judge and deliverer. In a decisive battle against his Midianite enemies, Gideon triumphs with only three hundred men (a witness to the triumph of Jesus' meek and solitary life). That victory is achieved first with a breaking (of jars), then a shining (of torches) and shout:

> For the Lord and for Gideon. (Jgs 7)

Death is effected and resurrection declared! Another judge, Samson, foretells Jesus' death and resurrection in a riddle-me-this manner. In Judges 14, Samson enters "Philistine" territory, desiring to obtain a wife. This event foretells the incarnation and its purpose in this godless age—Jesus has come to get His bride, the church. In his journey to gain that wife, Samson encounters a lion (Satan), which he kills. Then in the carcass of that lion (the death event between the Messiah and Satan), bees make honey. This honey becomes the subject of a riddle:

> Out of the eater came something to eat. Out of the strong came something sweet.

Does anything "eat" humanity more thoroughly than death? And yet there is one death which brings us "honey," God's sweet nourishment. It is found in the death of the Messiah in His conquest of Satan. His death is honey to a believer's soul. Can you answer the riddle? Those who do are clothed in proper attire for Samson's future wedding, clothing which Samson himself acquires and gives (cf. Rv 19:7–8)!

The psalms frequently bear witness to Jesus' resurrection. To cite a few:

- *Psalm 2 NIV.* The nations "take their stand" against the Lord and His anointed (death), but the Lord scoffs at them and proclaims, "You are my Son, today I have become your Father" (= the resurrection [cf. Acts 13:33]).
- *Psalm 16:9–11 NIV.* "You will not abandon me to the grave, nor will you let your Holy One see decay [death]… You have made known to me the path of life; you will fill me with joy in your presence" (= the resurrection [cf. Acts 2:25–28]).
- *Psalm 22 NIV.* The Scripture prophesies that the Messiah will cry in his heart, "I am poured out like water, and all my bones are out of joint: my heart has turned to wax; it has melted away within me…you lay me in the dust of death" (vv. 14–15). But that is not the end, for later in that same psalm, the Messiah testifies that, "I will declare your name to my brothers; in the congregation I will praise you…all the earth will remember and turn to the Lord" (vv. 22, 27).
- *Psalm 40:1–3 NIV.* "I waited patiently for the Lord; he turned to me and heard my cry. He lifted me out of the slimy pit, out of the mud and mire; he set my feet on a rock and gave me a firm place to stand. He put a new song in my mouth, a hymn of praise to our God. Many will see and fear and put their trust in the Lord." Witness to the resurrection is read throughout the psalms—cf. Pss 49, 118, 35 and, as quoted earlier, "Weeping may last through the night, but joy comes in the morning!"

For this reason, when the apostles "certified" Jesus' death and resurrection, they did so not only from their personal experience of meeting the *risen* Jesus, they did so foremostly "according to the Scriptures" (referring to the Old Testament).

> For I delivered to you as of first importance what I also received: that Christ died for sins in accordance with the Scriptures, that he was buried, that he was raised on the third day in accordance with the Scriptures, that he appeared to Cephas, then to the twelve. (1 Cor 15:3–5; emphases mine)

In our day, as evidence for the resurrection of Jesus, we commonly cite the empty tomb, the changed lives of the apostles from fear to boldness, the eyewitness of women, or the eventual martyrdom of the apostolic band and other early Christians (would they die for a lie?). However, it is incumbent to also mention as witness of the resurrection the entire Old Testament narrative. Jesus has fulfilled it, ushering in the New Covenant and, in His resurrection, ushering in a new narrative for the people who belong to Him.

Resurrection Identity

Indeed, this is the gospel! Through repentance and faith, Christians begin today a new identity as those who are "risen in Christ."

> In him (Christ) also you were circumcised with a circumcision made without hands, by putting off the body of the flesh, by the circumcision of Christ, having been buried with him in baptism, in which you were also raised with him through faith in the powerful working of God, who raised him from the dead. (Col 2:11–12)

Therefore, "if anyone is in Christ, he is a new creation; the old is gone, the new has come!" (2 Cor 5:17). It is the calling of the Christian, therefore, to live in and into this new identity.

> We were buried therefore with him by baptism
> into death, in order that, just as Christ was raised
> from the dead by the glory of the Father, we too
> might walk in newness of life. (Rom 6:4)

In Jesus *risen*, a Christian gains a vision of their future self toward which to live. "Since, then, you have been raised with Christ, set your hearts on things above, where Christ is seated at the right hand of God" (Col 3:1).

The resurrection identity therefore lifts a Christian all the way to become a "citizen of heaven" (Phil 3:20), even now in this age. By faith, a Christian lives along the Christ plotline through death into resurrection life.

> And God raised us up with Christ and seated us
> with him in the heavenly realms in Christ Jesus,
> in order that in the coming ages he might show
> the incomparable riches of his grace, expressed
> in his kindness to us in Christ Jesus. (Eph 2:6–7
> NIV)

This verse includes the second part of Jesus' glorification namely, His ascension into the heavenly realm. But before examining some scriptural witnesses to Jesus' ascension and our heavenly citizenship in Christ, for the sake of living in our new identity, it is helpful to understand the nature of Jesus' resurrected self.

Resurrection Nature

The resurrection accounts in the gospels make it very clear that Jesus was raised physically from the dead. His was a glorified physical body. In His resurrected self, Jesus ate with His disciples (Luke 24:41–43) and invited them to touch Him:

> See my hands and my feet, that it is I myself.
> Touch me, and see. For a spirit does not have
> flesh and bones as you see that I have. (Luke
> 24:39)

In His resurrection, Jesus' physical self was redeemed, just as a believer is promised bodily redemption at the glorification of all creation (Rom 8:22–23) in the general resurrection to come. Job articulates this hope, shared in Christ:

> For I know that my Redeemer lives, and at the
> last he will stand upon the earth. And after my
> skin has been thus destroyed yet in my flesh I
> shall see God. (Jb 19:25–26)

To be sure, Jesus' glorified physical self had abilities beyond that of our bodies in this current age of the earth. After His resurrection, Jesus could travel effortlessly and appear and disappear at will. While He could eat and drink and sit and talk, He also could go through walls and doors (Jn 20:19–20). On the Mount of Transfiguration, when Jesus conversed with Moses and Elijah about His upcoming death, Peter, James, and John were given a glimpse of Jesus' glorified self.

> The appearance of his face was altered, and his
> clothing became dazzling white. (Luke 9:29)

Surely this experience encouraged Jesus in His journey to the cross, promising His glory beyond it.

Jesus' resurrected self is the "first-fruit" of both the Christian's promised bodily resurrection and creation's promised physical glorification (1 Cor 15:23). In the day of Jesus' triumphant return, "all who are in the tombs will hear his voice and come forth" (Jn 5:28).

In that Great Day, when this age of the earth finds its consummation and fulfillment, some will be "resurrected to life," others "resurrected to condemnation" (Jn 5:29). For those in Christ,

> the body that was sown perishable will be raised imperishable; the body sown in dishonor will be raised in glory; sown in weakness will be raised in power; sown a natural body, raised a spiritual body. (1 Cor 15:42–44 NIV)

Spiritual here is referring to a glorified physical body completely responsive to the Holy Spirit.

The physicality of the believer's future resurrected body is significant for his/her living today. The physical world matters. We should not think of our heavenly life as "otherworldly." That is Platonic and Gnostic teaching, not from the Bible. Scripturally, material reality is good. Therefore, we are called to "glorify God in our bodies" (1 Cor 6:20) and to "cleanse ourselves from everything that contaminates body and spirit, perfecting holiness out of reverence for God" (2 Cor 7:1). As we live toward our future selves and world, we learn to enjoy and care for the body and all our material world. Humans are material beings, always.

Beyond this, we also see in Jesus' resurrected body an organic relationship between our physical self in this age and ours in the next. Jesus showed His disciples the crucifixion marks on His resurrected body (Jn 20:20). Those markings from His preresurrected body continued to be part of His resurrected self. He was not a completely different person. Jesus' physical "story" in one age continues on in fulfillment in the next (as does also His "spiritual story," Heb 5:7–10). There was a physical translation, yes, but there were also measures of continuity. As on the Road to Emmaus walk with two of His disciples, sometimes Jesus was not physically recognized (Luke 24:16), but then later He would be (24:31). The same happened to Mary Magdalene the first Easter morning (Jn 20:10–18).

This organic unity between this age and the next can be likened to the Old and New Covenants of Scripture (Jer 31:31–34). There is both continuity and discontinuity. There is also fulfillment of the Old in the New. So, too, is the relationship of this age of the earth with the next, the new earth. The "glory and honor of the nations" (Rv 21:26) from this age will be brought into the next age of the earth. What material and cultural affirmation!

Another analogy, one that Jesus Himself alludes to in Matthew 24:8, is the organic physical unity between a mother and child. Jesus likens His kingdom's presence in this world as a child in the womb of her mother. This analogy will serve us more fully later in this book. But suffice it to say that while a child is uniquely her own person, yet she bears definite semblances to her mother, such that at times, that relationship is easily recognized, at other times not. In the meantime, while a child is yet physically in the womb of her mother, the mother's physical health is to be nurtured and cherished. Even so, as a believer lives toward the future Resurrection Day, his/her physical self and world is to be enjoyed and cared for.

CHAPTER 8

Glorification: Ascension

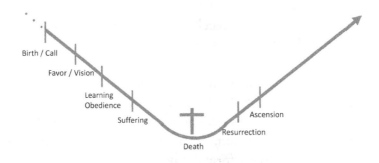

Birth / Call

Favor / Vision

Learning
Obedience

Suffering

Ascension

Resurrection

Death

The Ascension

The exaltation of Jesus Christ is a two-stage affair. After the resurrection, Jesus is exalted to the right hand of the heavenly Father in His public ascension.

> But you will receive power when the Holy Spirit
> has come upon you, and you will be my witnesses
> in Jerusalem and in all Judea and Samaria, and to
> the end of the earth. (Acts 1:8–9)

The Bible makes very clear that together with His resurrection, this ascension event is Jesus' coronation as "King of kings" (1 Tm 6:15).

> He who sits in the heavens laughs; the Lord holds them in derision. Then he will speak to them in his wrath, and terrify them in his fury, saying, "As for me, I have set my King on Zion, my holy hill." (Ps 2:4–6)

In the heavenlies, this coronation is a grand event:

> You ascended on high, leading a host of captives in your train and receiving gifts among men, even among the rebellious, that the Lord God may dwell there. (Ps 68:18)

In terms of the American government, Jesus' resurrection was His *election* to God's Oval Office (in November every four years), His ascension was His *inauguration* into that office (the following January). Upon inauguration, the president formally begins his rule. Even so, Jesus' ascension formally begins His rule on earth at the "right hand" of God Almighty (Ps 110), the right hand being a symbol of the power and action of God's rule on earth. In the next chapter, we will explore the scriptural witness and meaning of Jesus' reign on earth. For the remainder of this chapter, let's recognize some of the scriptural witnesses to Jesus' ascension and the Christian's ascended life in Him.

> If then you have been raised with Christ, seek the things that are above, where Christ is, seated at the right hand of God. (Col 3:1)

One of the earliest scriptural witnesses of the messianic journey (the Christ plotline) is in the call of Abram in Genesis 12:1–8. This is the cardinal story of Abram's life, one fulfilled in Jesus.

Abram is called to "leave his country, his father's household" (even as the Eternal Son left His heavenly home and Father) so that he might become a great nation and a divider of humanity—whoever blesses him is blessed, whoever curses him is cursed (v. 3). This call takes him into the land of Canaan (which eventually becomes the promised land—i.e., the new earth). Once there, Abram travels to the "Great Tree of Moreh" (the cross) at which God confirms that Abram's offspring will inherit that land and at which an altar is built (signifying the sacrificial/intercessory nature of the cross). Thereafter, Abram "ascends to the hills and pitched his tent" (the messianic exaltation), and Abram there builds a second altar to "call on the name of the Lord" (v. 8). This ascended altar bears witness to Jesus as our heavenly mediator.

> Who is to condemn? Christ Jesus is the one who
> died—more than that, who was raised—who is
> at the right hand of God, who indeed is interced-
> ing for us. (Rom 8:34)

Another messianic journey closely related to Abram's is the high priest's journey in temple ministry, particularly on the Day of Atonement. That journey begins outside of the temple proper (i.e., in this sin-stained age of the earth), at the altar of sacrifice—the altar where blood is shed to make atonement for sin (i.e., the cross). Thereafter cleansed (at the laver), the high priest enters the temple's Holy Place (the heavenlies) with its table of showbread, lampstand, and altar of incense. Then on the Day of Atonement, that journey continues with blood into the Holy of Holies, past the dividing curtain, to the ark of the covenant. In Jesus, however, that dividing curtain has been torn down (Luke 23:45). So He has entered the Holy of Holies once for all, seated at the right hand of God.

> Jesus went through the greater and more perfect
> tabernacle that is not man-made, that is to say,
> not a part of this creation. He did not enter by
> means of the blood of goats and calves; but he

97

> entered the most Holy Place once for all by his
> own blood, having obtained eternal redemption.
> (Heb 9:11–12 NIV)

Ascended into the heavenlies, therefore, Jesus ministers at the Covenant God's right hand as the Light of the World (Lampstand), the Bread of Life (Table), and the Great High Priestly Intercessor (Altar of Incense).

One other Old Testament journey that foretells Jesus' ascension centers on the ark of the covenant, the symbol of the Lord's presence with His people. In the days when the prophet Samuel was beginning his ministry, this ark was treated like a talisman and hauled out to the battlefield in Israel's conflict with the Philistines (1 Sm 4). So mistreated by its own people (Jesus rejected), the ark was captured by the Philistines (the "defeat" of the cross) and brought into foreign territory ("He descended into hell"). There in the land of the Philistines, the ark declares God's lordship over rival gods (Dagon falls on his face before the ark [1 Sm 5:2] and, eventually, his head and hands are broken off). There, too, in that foreign land, the ark curses the enemies of God (= the triumph of Jesus' death over evil).

> Death filled the Philistine city with panic. God's
> hand was very heavy upon it. Those who did not
> die were afflicted with tumors, and the outcry of
> the city went up to heaven. (1 Sm 5:11–12 NIV)

Then by the power of a miracle (mother cows leaving their newborn young), the ark is returned with tribute to the promised land (= Jesus' resurrection). It ends up first in the town of Beth Shemesh where its sacredness is not respected, even among those who are part of God's covenant people. The men there are struck down dead, 50,070 of them (1 Sm 6:19). Beware lest the Resurrected One be treated with triviality! Then the ark settles near to Jerusalem at the house of Abinadab in Kiriath Jearim. Having singularly defeated the Philistine powers, the ark remains at Kiriath Jearim for twenty years.

In its presence, the prophet Samuel ministers the Word of God (resurrection preaching):

> Samuel said to the whole house of Israel, "If you are returning to the Lord with all your hearts, then rid yourselves of the foreign gods and the Ashtoreths and commit yourselves to the Lord and serve him only, and he will deliver you out of the hands of the Philistines." So the Israelites put away their Baals and Ashtoreths, and served the Lord only. (1 Sm 7:3–4 NIV)

Then comes the "ascension movement" in this story. After twenty years in Kiriath Jearim during which David becomes king and establishes Jerusalem as his capital city, he decides to install the ark in its rightful place of glory—in the Royal City—and to place it temporarily in a tent until a temple be built for it. A grand procession is planned for, in worship and music. The ascension begins but quickly grinds to a halt when one of the sons of Abinadab, Uzzah, irreverently places his hand on the ark to steady it while it travels on a cart. Uzzah dies doing so, and David learns that the ark is only to be transported with poles by those of Levitical lineage. Three months later, the procession is obediently undertaken with joy and celebration, prayer and sacrifice, David leading the procession, "dancing before the Lord with all his might" (2 Sm 6:14). This time, the ark enters Jerusalem, and with the presence of God established in its royal place, David distributes gifts to all God's people, men and women. He gives cakes of dates and cakes of raisins (v. 19). Quoting from Psalm 68:18, the apostle Paul comments on this element of the ascension:

> But to each one of us grace has been given as Christ apportioned it. This is why it says: "When he ascended on high, he led captives in his train and gave gifts to men." What does "he ascended" mean except that he also descended to the depths

of the earth. He who descended is the very one who ascended higher than all the heavens in order to fill the whole universe. (Eph 4:7–10 NIV)

Besides Psalm 68, there are numerous other psalms that bear witness to Jesus' ascension and its meaning as His King of kings coronation. These psalms are readily and naturally read in Christ. Psalm 132 is a "song of ascent" that envisions Jesus' ascension and ministry therefrom:

> The Lord has chosen Zion, he has desired it for his dwelling: "This is my resting place forever and ever; here I will sit enthroned, for I have desired it—I will bless her with abundant provisions; her poor will I satisfy with food. I will clothe her priests with salvation, and her saints will ever sing for joy. Here I will make a horn grow for David and set up a lamp for my anointed one. I will clothe his enemies with shame, but the crown on his head will be resplendent." (Ps 132:13–18 NIV)

Who is worthy of such exaltation? Jesus, alone and derivatively, and those in Christ:

> Who may ascend the hill of the Lord? Who may stand in his holy place? He who has clean hands and a pure heart, who does not lift up his soul to an idol or swear by what is false. He will receive blessing from the Lord and vindication from God his Savior. (Ps 24:3–4 NIV)

Psalm 110 is the most quoted piece of writing cited in the New Testament from the Old:

> The Lord says to my Lord: "Sit at my right hand until I make your enemies a footstool for your

feet." The Lord will extend your mighty scepter from Zion; you will rule in the midst of your enemies. Your troops will be willing on your day of battle. (Ps 110:1–3 NIV)

Psalm 2 is quoted in Hebrews 1:5 as referring to Jesus' ascension to the right hand of God Almighty:

He said to me, "You are my Son; today I have become your Father. Ask of me and I will make the nations your inheritance and the ends of the earth your possession"… Therefore you kings be wise; be warned, you rulers of the earth. Serve the Lord with fear and rejoice with trembling. Kiss the Son, lest he be angry and you be destroyed in your way, for his wrath can flare up in a moment. Blessed are all who take refuge in him. (Ps 2:7–12 NIV)

Psalm 47 takes us into the heavenly joys of Jesus' ascension:

God has ascended amid shouts of joy, the Lord amid the soundings of trumpets. Sing praise to God, sing praises. For God is the king of all the earth; sing to him a psalm of praise. God reigns over the nations; God is seated on his holy throne. The nobles assemble of the nations as the people of the God of Abraham, for the kings of the earth belong to God; he is greatly exalted. (Ps 47 NIV)

Before turning to Jesus' current reign on earth as King of kings, let's also note some individual Old Testament witnesses to His ascension and His glory therein. In chapter 1, we chronicled Joseph's story, one which portrays most aspects of the Christ plotline. Having interpreted the Pharaoh's dreams (Gn 41), Joseph is raised out of prison and exalted to the right hand of Pharaoh, "put in charge of the whole land of Egypt" (v. 41). Likewise, Daniel is delivered out of the lions' den, and in his exaltation, he is set by King Darius "over the whole of his kingdom" (Dn 6:3). In that deliverance, Daniel's rivals are consumed by those same lions, and King Darius writes to all peoples, nations, and men of every language through his land,

> I make a decree, that in all my royal dominion people are to tremble and fear before the God of Daniel, for he is the living God, enduring forever; his kingdom shall never be destroyed, and his dominion shall be to the end. (Dn 6:26)

In a lesser way, Enoch bears witness to the ascended Lord Jesus for

> Enoch walked with God, and he was not, for God took him. (Gn 5:24)

So, too, Elijah was translated into heavenly glory without the passage of physical death. Like the apostolic band present with Jesus at His ascension event, 2 Kings 2:11–12 NIV states,

> As Elijah and Elisha were walking along and talking together, suddenly a chariot of fire and horses of fire appeared and separated the two of them, and Elijah went up to heaven in a whirlwind. Elisha saw this and cried out, 'My father! My father! The chariots and horsemen of Israel!' And Elisha saw him no more.

And because of his faithfulness to Elijah, Elisha was given the messianic anointing of Elijah to continue divine ministry, even as those apostles were similarly anointed through Jesus at Pentecost.

David/Solomon

King Solomon, too, must be recognized as someone who, in the Old Testament, prefigures the ascended Jesus. Solomon is a king of glory. In his day, he was the king of kings. He is a king of unmatched learning and wisdom.

> And people of all nations came to hear the wisdom of Solomon, and from all the kings of the earth, who had heard of his wisdom. (1 Kgs 4:34)

He is a king of unmatched wealth.

> Thus King Solomon excelled all the kings of the earth in riches and in wisdom. And the whole earth sought the presence of Solomon to hear his wisdom, which God had put into his mind. (1 Kgs 10:23–24)

Solomon became this great king because, like Jesus in preparation for His ascended rule, Solomon sought wisdom above all. In prayer, Solomon asked God,

> Give your servant therefore an understanding mind to govern your people, that I may discern between good and evil, for who is able to govern this your great people? (1 Kgs 3:9)

In response, God said to him,

> Since you have asked for this and not for long life or wealth for yourself, nor have asked for the death of your enemies but for discernment in administering justice, I will do what you have asked. I will give you a wise and discerning heart, so that there will never have been anyone like you, nor will there ever be. Moreover, I will give you what you have not asked for—both riches and honor—so that in your lifetime you will have no equal among kings. (1 Kgs 3:11–13 NIV)

Read in Christ, these words draw us into the humility and servant heart of Jesus. He became incarnate truly that He might gain the wisdom needed to guide God's people in this age, wisdom acquired even through suffering and death. Therefore, God has exalted Him so that there is no equal to Him among all kings.

Above all, Solomon bears witness to the exalted King Jesus because He is the king designated to build the temple of God on earth. This calling is understood in conjunction with Solomon's father, David. When he was king, David desired to build that temple for God, but he was not permitted.

> David said to Solomon: "My son, I had it in my heart to build a house for the Name of the Lord my God. But this word of the Lord came to me: 'You have shed much blood and have fought many wars. You are not to build a house for my Name, because you have shed much blood on the earth in my sight. But you will have a son who will be a man of peace and rest, and I will give him rest from all his enemies on every side. His name will be Solomon [i.e., shalom/peace]. He is the one who will build a house for my Name. He will be my son and I will be his father. And I will establish the throne of his kingdom over Israel forever.'" (1 Chr 22:7 NIV)

This text is quoted at length because it makes clear that David—the man of blood—is a type of Jesus in his earthly ministry, fighting wars, defeating Satan, and Solomon ("David II") is a type of Jesus in his exalted ministry, the one who is now building a temple on earth to the glory of God (cf. 1 Pt 2:4–10). And while it is Solomon who builds this *dwelling place* of God, it is David who acquires all the resources needed to do the job (1 Chr 22:14–16). It was in His state of "humiliation" that Jesus acquired the resources of obedience and wisdom, of grace and truth needed to build the new covenant temple (God's people, His dwelling place) by the power of the Spirit in His "exalted" state. As Solomon stands in relation to his father, David, so stands the exalted Jesus in relation to his earthly life.

Understood this way, we have a tremendous witness of the ascended glory of Jesus when the queen of Sheba visits King Solomon. It is the story of a seeker coming to know Jesus today. In 1 Kings 10:1–13, the queen comes to Solomon because she had heard about his fame, and she came to test him with hard questions. Solomon answered all her questions and proved his wisdom. As time went on, the queen also was given to see Solomon's palace, table, his officials, his cupbearers, his worship, his temple.

> The report I heard in my own country about your achievements and your wisdom is true. But I did not believe these things until I came and saw with my own eyes. Indeed, not even half was told me; in wisdom and wealth you have far exceeded the report I heard. How happy your men must be!... Because of the Lord's eternal love for Israel, he has made you king, to maintain justice and righteousness. (1 Kgs 10:6–9 NIV)

In response,

> King Solomon gave the queen of Sheba all she desired and asked for, besides what he had given her out of his royal bounty. (1 Kgs 10:13 NIV)

Indeed, "delight yourself in the Lord and he will give you the desires of your heart" (Ps 37:4).

CHAPTER 9

Reign: Nature and Agency

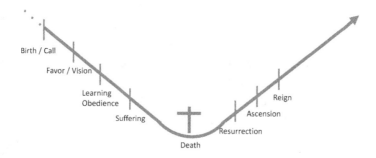

For unto us a child is born, unto us a son is given, And the government will be upon his shoulders. And he will be called Wonderful Counselor, Mighty God, Everlasting Father, Prince of Peace. Of the increase of his government and peace there will be no end. He will reign on David's throne and over his kingdom, Establishing and upholding it with justice and righteousness from that time on and forever. The zeal of the Lord Almighty shall accomplish this.
—Isaiah 9:6–7 NIV

If there's a neglected aspect of contemporary Christian orthodoxy, it has to be in understanding the reign of Jesus the Christ in our day of this age of the earth. Even in our historic creeds—the Apostles', Nicene, and Athanasian—there's an aching silence on this subject.

In them, Jesus' resurrection and ascension (coronation) is affirmed. But thereafter comes the immediate declaration that He shall "return to judge the living and the dead." But what is Jesus doing now as King of kings? Is He sitting *on* God's right hand of power and action (as a traditional version of the Apostles' Creed puts it)? No! He is sitting *at* that right hand because He is active and powerful, building an eternal kingdom on earth. In fact, Jesus *is* the right hand of God.

> The right hand of the Lord does valiantly, the right hand of the Lord exalts. (Ps 118:15)

Jesus is reigning today on earth, in and through His kingdom, the government of which brings God's shalom, justice, and righteousness into this age of the earth, a shalom which will be "from this time on and forever." Hence, the joy of Handel's *Messiah*.

> The kingdom of this world has become the kingdom of our Lord and of his Christ, and he will reign forever and ever. (Rv 11:15)

This is the preaching of the apostle Peter on the day of Pentecost. Quoting Psalm 110:1 as witness to Jesus' ascension,

> The Lord says to my Lord: "Sit at my right hand, until I make your enemies your footstool." (Ps 110:1)

Peter declares,

> Let all the house of Israel therefore know for certain that God has made him both Lord and Christ, this Jesus whom you crucified. (Acts 2:36)

Likewise, the apostle Paul teaches the current (not just future) reign of Jesus on earth in his chapter on the resurrection, 1 Corinthians 15.

> But Christ has indeed been raised from the dead, the firstfruits of those who have fallen asleep... For as in Adam all die, so in Christ all will be made alive. But each in his own turn: Christ, the firstfruits; then, when he comes those who belong to him. Then the end will come, when he hands over the kingdom to God the Father after he has destroyed all dominion, authority and power. For he must reign until he has put all his enemies under his feet. The last enemy to be destroyed is death. (1 Cor 15:20, 22–26 NIV)

Note here that death is the *last* enemy to be destroyed (referring to death, yes, physically and in all its meanings—physical, spiritual separation, warning, invitation, calling, passage). Some in the church teach that death is the first enemy to be destroyed (at Jesus' return), and then Jesus will begin His reign on earth. That is not the apostolic understanding of Jesus' current reign on earth (and a believer's reign in Christ). It is now and forever, in this current "Day of Salvation" (2 Cor 6:2). This accords with Jesus' own declaration:

> All authority in heaven and on earth has been given to me. Therefore go and make disciples of all nations, baptizing them in the name of the Father and of the Son and of the Holy Spirit, and teaching them to obey everything I have commanded you. And surely I am with you always, to the very end of the age. (Mt 28:16–20 NIV)

Jesus now reigns in His ascended glory at the right hand of God, a place not to be thought of as far away. He is in the heavens nearby, as present as the turn of a fifth dimension—just outside of space and time. In Him the veil between earth and heaven is thin. And as King, He has been exalted to reign on earth both personally and globally.

The Nature of Jesus' Reign

Jesus began His ministry by proclaiming this good news of God:

> The time is fulfilled, and the kingdom of God is at hand; repent and believe in the gospel. (Mk 1:15)

The King has come! Jesus Christ reigns in and through His kingdom on earth. Therefore, Jesus invited people to *enter* God's kingdom by becoming His followers (Mk 1:16–20). And He *bore witness* to the character of God's kingdom through His works of mercy and healing, teaching and preaching. These two complementary aspects of kingdom ministry, entrance and witness, constitute the nature of Jesus' reign on earth.

To enter the kingdom of God is to begin a life under God's *kingship*, His "rule" in Jesus Christ. It is a relationship with Jesus as Savior and Lord, a relationship in "spirit and truth" (Jn 4:24). When the rich young ruler asked Jesus what he must do to enter eternal life (Mt 19:16–24), after confronting this ruler with a proud identity in his own spiritual and material riches, Jesus then invited him also to become His follower. Sadly, the man refused.

> Blessed are the poor in spirit, for theirs is the kingdom of heaven. (Mt 5:3)

This man was full of himself, but the kingdom is opened to those who empty themselves in order to become, as a follower, full of God's life in Jesus. As the King of God's kingdom, we enter heavenly life through becoming a disciple of Jesus, who is the "gate for the sheep" (Jn 10:7). Through Him, we are reconciled to God, His death making atonement for our sin. And by His resurrection, we are raised to new kingdom life, eternal life in His Spirit and truth.

The other aspect of Jesus' kingdom ministry was in His works which bore witness both to Himself as King and to the character of God's kingdom which has begun in Him. This is the kingdom which "is and is to come," the now and not yet. In the Gospel of John, these works of witness are called signs. John highlights seven of these signs in the structure of his gospel but adds these words toward its end:

> Now Jesus did many other signs in the pres-
> ence of the disciples, which are not written in
> this book; but these are written so that you may
> believe that Jesus is the Christ, the Son of God,
> and that by believing you may have life in his
> name. (Jn 20:30–31)

Signs are pointers. Jesus' kingdom works pointed both to Himself as King and to the nature of God's kingdom itself. For example, He raised Lazarus from the dead to reveal to mankind that He is the "resurrection and the life" (Jn 11:25) and, further, to reveal that in God's kingdom, "death shall be no more" (Rv 21:4, Is 25:8). Likewise, Jesus fed the hungry (Jn 6:1–13) both to draw people to Himself as the Bread of Life (Jn 6:35) so that they might turn to Him in faith and *enter* the kingdom and also to point people toward God's kingdom wherein there is full provision for our every need—"He who comes to me will never go hungry." Jesus did not remove food as a sign of the kingdom; He provided food, for there is not scarcity but abundance in God's shalom kingdom.

> On this mountain the Lord of hosts will make for
> all peoples a feast of rich food, a feast of well-aged
> wine, of rich food full of marrow, of aged wine
> well refined. (Is 25:6)

Jesus healed the sick both because He is the Great Physician (Luke 5:31) and to reveal that in God's kingdom, there is fullness of health. Jesus made the lame to walk because there is ability in the new creation to move and explore and serve and work. Jesus made the deaf and dumb to communicate because in God's kingdom, there is ability to express ourselves to the glory of God and in works of love to others. Jesus delivered the demonized and oppressed because there is dignity and value for each person in God's kingdom. His works point to the character and nature of the kingdom and, in this, ultimately point to the new earth to come (Rv 21:1). Through His follower Zacchaeus (Luke 19:1–10), Jesus restored property to those who had been subject to extortion because in God's kingdom, there is justice and safety and rights to property.

> They shall sit every man under his vine and under his fig tree, and no one shall make them afraid. (Mi 4:4)

Jesus gave sight to the blind (Luke 18:42), both to draw people to Himself as the Light of the world and to reveal that in God's "now and not yet" kingdom, there is vision and knowledge.

> For the earth will be filled with the knowledge of the glory of the Lord as the waters cover the sea. (Hb 2:14)

> Come, let us go up to the mountain of the Lord, to the house of the God of Jacob, that he may teach us his ways and that we may walk in his paths. (Is 2:3)

Jesus' ministry was to proclaim that *in Him,* heaven had begun on earth. He invited people into that heavenly life through relationship with Himself as Savior and King. In Him then, people begin to taste the goodness of God's rule. Further, Jesus sought to bear witness to the goodness of God's kingdom through deeds as *signs* of the kingdom (whether those deeds be *miraculous* or not, something which can be hard to determine, a matter that ultimately makes little difference). These signs give others a taste of God's future on earth, drawing them to King Jesus and to heavenly life in Himself. They, too, give a vision of the new earth, a vision to live toward.

The Agency of Jesus' Reign

On the occasion of His ascension to the right hand of God the Father, Jesus made clear the agency of His reign on earth. To His followers, He said,

> Do not leave Jerusalem, but wait for the gift my Father promised, which you have heard me speak about… You will receive power when the Holy Spirit comes on you; and you will be my witnesses in Jerusalem, and in all Judea and Samaria, and to the ends of the earth. (Acts 1:4, 8 NIV)

The Holy Spirit living in the disciples of Jesus is the means by which He exercises His kingdom reign on earth.

This agency of the Spirit in Christ's people is anticipated in the Old Testament. One clear testimony to it is Ezekiel's vision of the Valley of Dry Bones (Ez 37). In chapter 36, Ezekiel had declared a day coming when God would

> give you a new heart and put a new spirit in you, removing your heart of stone and giving you a heart of flesh; putting my Spirit in you and moving you to follow my decrees and keep my laws; living in the land I gave your forefathers. (Ez 36:26–28 NIV)

Then in Ezekiel 37, the prophet is given to see a valley full of bones and asked (v. 3), "Son of man, can these bones live?" Subsequently, through the proclamation of God's Word, the bones come together, tendons and flesh cover them, but "there was no breath in them." Then once again the prophet proclaims the Word of God, and "breath entered them; they came to life and stood up on their feet—a vast ARMY" (v. 10). This is the day of Pentecost anticipated when the breath of God entered the followers of Jesus (Acts 2:1–2), and they became Christ's kingdom army, agents of His reign on earth. Thus Spirit-anointed, the apostle Peter explains, quoting Joel 2:28–32, that Jesus' people "see visions, dream dreams, and prophesy" (Acts 2:17), inviting others to enter the kingdom by "calling on the name of the Lord" (v. 21).

During His earthly ministry, Jesus Himself served God in the same power of the Spirit (Luke 4:14). But it was not until He had completed his life of obedience—through death, resurrection, and ascension—that He was able to release that same anointing of the Spirit into His people. This is explained in John 7:37–39. Jesus proclaims in a loud voice,

> If anyone is thirsty, let him come to me and drink. Whoever believes in me, as the Scripture has said, streams of living water will flow from within him. (Jn 7:37–39 NIV)

The gospel writer, John, explains after that,

> By this he meant the Spirit, whom those who believed in him were later to receive. Up to that time the Spirit had not been given, since Jesus had not yet been glorified.

Once glorified in His resurrection and ascension, heaven's vaults of Spirit life are opened wide to be released through Him into His people, to lead them into the same life of kingdom obedience and witness. This Spirit relationship between Jesus and His people is foreshadowed in Old Testament "couplings" such as Jacob and Joseph, Moses and Joshua, David and Solomon—the latter person "doing greater things" (Jn 14:12–14) than the former. The clearest Old Testament "coupling type" of the Spirit anointing of Jesus and then His followers is Elijah and Elisha. Elisha is called by Elijah to become his follower (1 Kgs 19:19–21). Elisha begins to learn kingdom ministry in following Elijah. But it is not until Elijah is "glorified" that Elisha is fully anointed by the Spirit. As Elijah approaches the day of his parting, he repeatedly tests Elisha's faithfulness as a follower (2 Kgs 2). Elisha responds,

> As the Lord lives, and as you yourself live, I will
> not leave you. (v 6)

This devotion continues through to their arrival at the Jordan River (emblem of death) which Elijah miraculously walks through (the resurrection) because of the power of his cloak (righteous obedience) with which he struck the water to divide it. Elisha travels through the Jordan River with Elijah, his own "death." "He who loses his life for my sake will find it" (Mt 16:25). On the other shore of death, Elijah asks Elisha, "What can I do for you?" Elisha replies,

> Please let there be a double portion of your spirit
> on me. (v 9)

(This is to continue kingdom ministry.) The request is granted on one condition. Elijah responds,

> If you see me as I am being taken from you, it
> shall be so for you. (v 10)

(To be anointed in the life of the Spirit, one must "see" the fullness of Jesus' glory.) Elisha does. He sees a chariot and horses of fire and Elijah assumed up to heaven in a whirlwind.

> My Father, my father! The chariots of Israel and
> its horsemen! (v 12)

Elisha cries out. This vision drafts him fully into the kingdom's military service. Thereupon, Elisha picks up Elijah's cloak, returns to the Jordan, and strikes the water with the mantle as Elijah had previously done. The water divides.

> O death, where is your victory? O death, where is
> your sting? (1 Cor 15:55)

The cloak of Jesus' righteousness has removed the power of sin and the sting of death. Thanks be to God for our victory in the Lord Jesus and the anointing of His Spirit.

> The saying is trustworthy, for: If we have died
> with him, we will also live with him; if we endure,
> we will also reign with him. (2 Tm 2:11–12)

This is how a Christian reads the Elijah-Elisha story in Christ, equipped by the Spirit to serve Jesus' reign on earth.

Other Old Testament references point to the agency of the Spirit and invite us to carry out the reign of Jesus by His power. In creation (Gn 1), it is through the agency of the Spirit that nature's order, beauty, and flourishing come about. In building the tabernacle and its furnishings, the Spirit fills Bezalel, son of Uri and Oholiab, son of Ahisamach, giving them (Ex 31:3–5 NIV).

> skill, ability and knowledge in all kinds of
> crafts—to make artistic designs for work in gold,
> silver and bronze, to cut and set stones, to work
> in wood, and to engage in all kinds of craftsman-
> ship. (Ex 31:1–11)

The Spirit "came upon" certain leaders for their work of service—Joshua (Nm 27:18), Saul (1 Sm 10:10), and David (1 Sm 16:12–13). In Israel's time of the judges, various deliverers, too, experience the power of the Spirit in their work of kingdom leadership. Samson is one such example (Jgs 15:14–15). Gideon is another (Jgs 6:34). Gideon's reliance on the Spirit is particularly noteworthy in his use of the wool fleece to ascertain God's leading (Jgs 6:36–30).

The messianic story is portrayed through this fleece testing. Gideon places the wool fleece on his threshing floor one night, requesting that in the morning the fleece be wet with dew and the ground around it dry. The next night, he requests the reverse, that the fleece be dry and ground wet. Both requests are granted by God. Dew being a symbol of the Spirit and sheep's fleece being a symbol of God's people, Gideon is asking on the first night for the sign that he is anointed by the Spirit to be Israel's deliverer. Then on the second night, he is asking that the Spirit be sent forth from him into the world to defeat the enemies of God. Ultimately, this points to the dual movements of Jesus' life. In His earthly life, Jesus was uniquely the "Man of the Spirit" (first night). Upon His death (the dry fleece), the Spirit is sent out through Jesus into the world to accomplish God's victorious kingdom purposes.

Prophet, Priest, and King

The present reign of the Ascended Jesus through the Holy Spirit in His followers should also be understood according to His three "offices" of ministry—Prophet, Priest, and King. Jesus is the *Christ*, meaning the "Anointed One" (in Hebrew, *Messiah* = Anointed One). This term has Old Testament roots as each of these three ministries were entered by means of an anointing with oil, symbolizing the empowering of the Spirit of God.

> Anoint Aaron and his sons, and consecrate them,
> that they may serve me as priests. (Ex 30:30)

This was God's command to Moses, the anointing oil being specially prepared (Ex 30:22–29). Likewise, kings were anointed into office.

> Then Samuel took a flask of oil and poured it on
> his head and kissed him and said, "Has not the
> Lord anointed you to be prince over his people
> Israel?" (1 Sm 10:1)

So, too, were prophets.

> The Lord said to Elijah, "Anoint Jehu son of
> Nimshi king over Israel, and anoint Elisha son
> of Shaphat from Abel Meholah to succeed you as
> prophet." (1 Kgs 19:16 NIV)

As the Christ then, Jesus is *the* anointed one who, in the New Covenant, fulfills these three Old Testament offices of ministry. As Messiah, He is the ultimate and true Prophet, Priest, and King. As He Himself announced, drawing from Isaiah 61:1–3,

> The Spirit of the Lord is upon me, because he has
> anointed me to proclaim good news to the poor.
> He has sent me to proclaim liberty to the cap-
> tives and recovering of sight to the blind, to set at
> liberty those who are oppressed, to proclaim the
> year of the Lord's favor. (Luke 4:18–19)

In its most fundamental sense, the ministry of a prophet is to bring "God to mankind," revealing His will. The ministry of a priest is to bring "mankind to God," effecting reconciliation and restoration of relationship. The ministry of a king is to "rule," governing with authority delegated from God. Hebrews 1:1–3 affirms Jesus as *the* Prophet, Priest, and King of God's new covenant.

> In the past God spoke to our forefathers through
> the prophets at many times and in various ways,
> but in these last days he has spoken to us by his
> Son [= the Prophet], whom he appointed heir of
> all things, and through whom he made the uni-
> verse. The Son is the radiance of God's glory and
> exact representation of his being, sustaining all
> things by his powerful word [= the King]. After
> he had provided purification for sins, he sat down

at the right hand of the Majesty in heaven [= the Priest]. (Heb 1:1–3 NIV)

In building His kingdom on earth, Jesus shares His priestly, kingly, and prophetic anointings with His people. This is the work of the Holy Spirit in and through the life of a Christian. This is how Jesus reigns on earth today.

> But the anointing that you received from him abides in you, and you have no need that anyone should teach you. But as his anointing teaches you about everything—and is true and is no lie, just as it has taught you—abide in him. (1 Jn 2:27)

This anointing is implied in Jesus' words from John 15:5:

> I am the vine; you are the branches. Whoever abides in me and I in him, he it is that bears much fruit, for apart from me you can do nothing.

Q and A 32 of the "Heidelberg Catechism" asks, "Why are you called a Christian?" and responds, "Because by faith I am a member of Christ and so I share in his anointing." In Christ then, Christian ministry is priestly, prophetic, and kingly. Therefore, in reading Scripture's priestly, prophetic, and kingly narratives, we are first drawn to Jesus as the ultimate Priest, Prophet, and King and, thereafter, are led to Christian ministry in Him.

Priest

In building His kingdom on earth, Jesus has become the Great High Priest of His people.

> One who is seated at the right hand of the throne of the Majesty in heaven, a minister in the holy

118

places, in the true tent that the Lord set up, not man. (Heb 8:1–2)

The purpose of this anointing is to "act on behalf of men in relation to God, to offer gifts and sacrifices for sins" (Heb 5:1). It is to "bring mankind to God" in intercession. To qualify for this office, the Eternal Son became incarnate. Jesus faced temptation so He could sympathize with our weakness (Heb 4:15); He offered prayers and supplications (Heb 5:7); He learned obedience through what He suffered (Heb 5:8), all the while remaining fully obedient, without sin. His full obedience meant that the sacrificing of His life and the offering of His blood makes full atonement for the sins of His people.

Through the anointing of Jesus' Spirit, Christians themselves become priests.

> But you are a chosen race, a royal priesthood, a holy nation, a people for his own possession, that you may proclaim the excellencies of him who called you out of darkness into his marvelous light. (1 Pt 2:9)

In Revelation 5:9–10 it says *worthy* is the Lamb because

> You have made them a kingdom and priests to our God, and they shall reign on the earth. (Rv 5:9–10)

Priestly ministry, therefore, in the anointing of the Spirit, "brings mankind to God." In Christ, it is accomplished through self-giving intercession for others. Like Jesus, it is done through learning obedience and gaining compassion for others, facing the temptations that they face, understanding the brokenness of sin in people and society. It is done through prayer and mercy and care for others. The same Spirit that matured Jesus into His High Priestly position anoints His people to be and become priests in this world, bringing others through the blood of Jesus into reconciliation with God and therein building Jesus' reign on earth.

Reading Scripture in Christ, we can then take to heart the priestly ministry of the Old Testament, both as it draws us to Jesus and to His priestly Spirit alive in us. There are great stories of intercession that foretell Jesus' intercessory ministry—Abraham for Lot (Gn 18:22–33) and Moses for the Israelites (Ex 17:8–16, 33:12–23). More clearly, Leviticus 9–10 bears witness of both true and false priestly ministry. The context is Moses' initiation of Aaron and his sons into their priestly work. Much of the book of Leviticus spells out proper and obedient priestly work in the Old Covenant context. In chapter 9 verse 6, Moses clarifies that this work is to be done as the Lord commands "so that the glory of the Lord may appear to you." And after Aaron and his sons perform their priestly ministry obediently,

> Aaron lifted his hands toward the people and blessed them, and he came down from offering the sin offering and the burnt offering and the peace offerings. And Moses and Aaron went into the tent of meeting, and when they came out they blessed the people, and the glory of the Lord appeared to all the people. And fire came out from before the Lord and consumed the burnt offering and the pieces of fat on the altar, and when all the people saw it, they shouted and fell on their faces. (Lv 9:22–24)

What testimony this is to the full obedience of Jesus who, on the cross, became our *sin and burnt and peace* (above) offering unto God, whose life and sacrifice was vindicated by its "consumption" in the resurrection, through whom the glory of God appeared to all people and before whom we "shout and fall on our faces."

Conversely, Leviticus 10 reveals disobedient priestly ministry in Aaron's sons, Nadab and Abihu.

> They each took his censer and put fire in it and laid incense on it and offered unauthorized fire

before the Lord, which he had not commanded
them. And fire came out from before the Lord
and consumed them and they died before the
Lord. (Lv 10:1–2)

What did Nadab and Abihu do so wrong that led to their death?
God had made clear that the only fire to be used in priestly ministry
was to be drawn from the brazen altar (cf. Lv 16:12). The brazen altar
was the altar of blood sacrifice located outside the temple proper.
From that altar was fire to be taken. Apparently, the "unauthorized
fire" that Nadab and Abihu offered was taken from another source.
In Christ, this reveals that there is one "fire," one "Spirit," one sacrifice in which we are to conduct priestly ministry—the blood sacrifice
of the crucified Jesus. His Spirit living in us conducts true priestly
ministry acceptable to God. The heart matters. Motives matter.
Hophni and Phinehas, the priestly sons of Eli, similarly were judged
unto death for their false lives. Malachi rebuked the priests of his day,

> Now, O priests, this command is for you. If you
> will not listen, if you will not take it to heart to
> give honor to my name, says the Lord of hosts,
> then I will send the curse upon you and I will
> curse your blessings. (Mal 2:1–2)

As priests in Christ, we take heed to those words by doing ministry in the Spirit of Jesus and to the honor of His name.

In the New Testament, the apostle Paul's priestly anointing in
Jesus is particularly revealed in his letter of Second Corinthians. Paul
writes to them for the sake of reconciliation and restoration of their
relationship, that they might live into the reconciliation that Jesus
has accomplished in relationship with God (2 Cor 5:11–6:13).

> The love of Christ controls us. (2 Cor 5:14)

> Our heart is wide open to you—in return widen
> your hearts also. (2 Cor 6:11, 13)

Paul opens his heart to the Corinthian congregation chiefly because God has opened His heart to us in Christ Jesus. As a priest in Christ, Paul also learns obedience through suffering:

> As servants of God we commend ourselves in every way: by great endurance in afflictions, hardships, calamities, beatings, imprisonments, riots, labors, sleepless nights, hunger; by purity, knowledge, patience, kindness, the Holy Spirit, genuine love, by truth speech, and the power of God. (2 Cor 6:4–7)

This obedience brings him the ministries of mercy and comfort:

> For as we share abundantly in Christ's sufferings, so through Christ we share abundantly in comfort too. If we are afflicted, it is for your comfort and salvation; and if we are comforted, it is for your comfort, which you experience when you patiently endure the same sufferings that we suffer. (2 Cor 1:5–6)

In all of this, Paul is serving in the intercessory spirit of Jesus, building Jesus' reign on earth:

> We are ambassadors for Christ, God making his appeal through us. We implore you on behalf of Christ, be reconciled to God. For our sake he made him to be sin who knew no sin, so that in him we might become the righteousness of God. (2 Cor 5:20–21)

Christian priests bring *mankind to God* in the Spirit of Jesus.

Prophet

Prophetic ministry brings *God to mankind*. It is knowing and proclaiming, teaching and sharing the will of God. It is counsel and evangelism and wisdom. It is rebuke and comfort. It is hope and judgment. Christian prophetic ministry is centered in Jesus who proclaimed that He is God's truth on earth. Through Him, God's will is definitively known, and through this ministry, Jesus extends His reign on earth.

In the Old Testament, Moses anticipated a definitive Prophet of God to come.

> The Lord your God will raise up for you a prophet like me from among you, from your brothers—it is to him you shall listen... And I will put my words in his mouth, and he shall speak to them all that I command him. And whoever will not listen to my words that he shall speak in my name, I myself will require it of him. (Dt 18:15, 18–19)

Jesus is this Prophet. He is the Eternal Word of God who was "with God and was God" (Jn. 1:1).

> The Word became flesh and dwelt among us, and we have seen his glory, glory as of the only Son from the Father, full of grace and truth. (Jn 1:14)

> Long ago, at many times and in many ways, God spoke to our fathers by the prophets, but in these last days he has spoken to us by his Son, whom he appointed the heir of all things, through whom also he created the world. (Heb 1:1–2)

In conjunction with His prophetic office, Jesus "taught with authority" (Mt 7:29). He claimed that everyone who builds their life on

His words builds upon a solid rock, but those who hear and do not obey His words are like the "foolish man who builds his house on the sand" (Mt 7:26). When the rains of judgment come, that house falls and "great was the fall of it" (v. 27). Jesus is God's truth on earth (Jn 14:6).

Christian *prophetic ministry* in the power of Jesus' anointing should not first be thought of in reference to gifts of prophecy or knowledge (1 Cor 12:8–10), nor to prophetic gifting in the five-fold leadership gifts for the church (Eph 4:11), though these gifts are extensions of it. More fundamentally, this ministry is about the discernment of God's will through the indwelling Spirit of Christ. First John 2:27 explains it:

> The anointing that you received from him abides in you, and you have no need that anyone should teach you. But as his anointing teaches you about everything—and is true and is no lie, just as it has taught you—abide in him.

By this, John is not dismissing teachers or preachers but referring to the inner witness of the Spirit to guide us into truth. The prophetic anointing of Jesus leads us to obey the command of Romans 12:2:

> Do not be conformed to this world, but be trans-formed by the renewal of your mind, that by testing you may discern what is the will of God, what is good and acceptable and perfect.

It is from this base of knowing God that Christians then gift into ministries of teaching, preaching, counsel, evangelism, calls for justice, words of comfort, bringing God's truth to people, families and society, extending the reign of Christ.

This Spirit-empowered prophetic ability was foretold in the Old Testament.

> But this is the (new) covenant I will make with the house of Israel after those days, declares the

Lord. I will put my law within them, and I will
write it on their hearts. And I will be their God,
and they shall be my people. And no longer shall
each one teach his neighbor and each his brother,
saying, "Know the Lord," for they shall all know
me from the least of them to the greatest, declares
the Lord. For I will forgive their iniquity, and I
will remember their sins no more. (Jer 31:33–34)

Through Jesus, this promise has been fulfilled. His Spirit leads
us into the sure knowledge of God.

When Moses declared in Deuteronomy 18 that God would
raise up a definitive messianic Prophet, he also warned against false
prophets who do not speak the word of the Lord (vv. 20–22). These
are prophets who "speak presumptuously," whose words do not come
to pass. Read in Christ, the Old Testament narratives of true versus
false prophets point to Jesus Christ, God's truth and salvation on
earth. Balaam was a prophet anointed with the Spirit of God (Nms
22–24). Though hired by Balak, king of Moab, to curse Israel in their
journey to the promised land, Balaam couldn't.

How can I curse whom God has not cursed?
How can I denounce whom the Lord has not
denounced? (Nm 23:8)

God brings him out of Egypt and is for him like
the horns of the wild ox. (Nm 24:8)

I see him, but not now; I behold him, but not
near: a star shall come out of Jacob, and a scepter
shall rise out of Israel; it shall crush the forehead
of Moab. (Nm 24:17)

And one from Jacob shall exercise dominion.
(Nm 24:19)

As witnessed here and stated in Revelation 19:10, "the testimony of Jesus is the spirit of prophecy."

That testimony is evidenced in Elijah's confrontation with the false prophets of Baal on Mount Carmel. When his altar offering (crucifixion) is completely consumed (resurrection) by fire from heaven (1 Kgs 18:38), the people cry, "ELI-JAH [= the Lord is God]," and the rains fall from the heavens (Pentecost, the Holy Spirit). Later, Ahab's false prophets are confronted by Micaiah, the "prophet of the Lord" (1 Kgs 22:7). His word condemns wicked Ahab to death, but it leads Micaiah himself to be struck on the cheek and imprisoned (vv. 24–28)—prophetic of Christ's sufferings, like the sufferings of so many prophets (Acts 7:52). First John 2:27 states that Jesus' prophetic anointing teaches us to "abide in Him" as we share God's truth with others. That truth leads to words of both judgment and grace. The holiness of God and the requirements of obedience are part and parcel of the truth of Jesus, in tandem with grace.

Prophetic ministry through the anointing of the Spirit is always centered in Jesus. He is the one who claimed,

> If you abide in my word, you are truly my disciples, and you will know the truth, and the truth will set you free. (Jn 8:31)

By sharing that truth of God, Jesus' reign on earth is furthered.

King

As Christ, Jesus is the anointed King of kings.

> He is the blessed and only Sovereign, the King of kings and Lord of lords who alone has immortality, who dwells in unapproachable light whom no one has ever seen or can see. To him be honor and eternal dominion. Amen. (1 Tm 6:15–16)

All authority in heaven and earth has been given to Him (Mt 28:18) with which to rule on earth, building his kingdom which is and is to come. In His rule, there is order and blessing, obedience and joy; there is safety and provision; there is wisdom and vision; there is holiness and love; there is knowledge and human flourishing. As King, Jesus implements God's good authority on earth.

That authority He also designates to His followers through the anointing of His Spirit. In Christ, believers are anointed for *kingly (or queenly) ministry.* This refers to godly rule on earth, the governance of God as man and man as vice-regents of God. Revelation 5:9–10 says worthy is the Lamb,

> For you were slain and by your blood you ransomed people for God from every tribe and language and people and nation and you have made them a kingdom and priests to our God, and they shall reign on the earth.

That reign, like Christ's kingdom itself, is both now and not yet, both "is and is to come." In preparing His followers for the day of His return, Jesus told the parable of the talents (Mt 25:14–30). The talents given represent differing measures of the Spirit, God's truth and love. For those who are faithful, cultivating and growing the life of the Spirit, they are "set over much" (v. 21) in the life to come. Leadership in Spirit life now will know its reward in the age to come. Luke's similar parable (Luke 19:11–27) makes this even more explicit. Those who have been faithful in Spirit governance are "set over five or ten cities."

> If we have died with him, we will also live with him; if we endure, we will also reign with him. (2 Tm 2:12)

The apostle Paul likewise recognizes that through Christ, we are set apart to reign on earth. In 1 Corinthians 6, he chastises the church because one member is taking another to public court.

> Do you not know that the saints will judge the world? And if the world is to be judged by you, are you incompetent to try trivial cases? Do you not know that we are to judge angels? How much more, then, matters pertaining to this life. I say this to your shame. (1 Cor 6:1–3, 5)

In Christ, Paul expects believers to gain the wisdom to judge and resolve issues of contention. This, too, is part of kingly ministry. Kingly ministry in Christ begins with self-governance.

> For God did not give you a spirit of fear, but of power and love and self-control. (2 Tm 1:7)

> The fruit of the Spirit is love, joy, peace, patience, kindness, goodness, faithfulness, gentleness, self-control; against such things there is no law. (Gal 5:22–23)

Along with self-governance, kingly ministry involves learning:

> It is the glory of God to conceal things, but the glory of kings to search things out. (Prv 25:2)

From this foundation of self-government, kingly ministry can grow into leadership in family life and then the church:

> An elder must manage his own household well, with all dignity keeping his children submissive, for if someone does not know how to manage his own household, how will he care for God's church? (1 Tm 3:4–5)

In this, kingly ministry involves disciplining others so that their lives are shaped in obedience and joy. It is using authority to serve and bless others. It is leading with humility and strength. Kingly ministry is leadership with the love of Christ.

Beyond family and church, this ministry manifests in leadership in community organizations, business ownership, workplace departments, sports teams, and broader governments of society. Because it leads others with the humility and strength of Christ, it brings them into flourishing and well-being. It manifests to others the shalom of God's kingdom which is and is to come. Above all, it points to Jesus as the King of kings and invites others to begin a life under His rule.

The Scriptures contain many stories of kings. Read in Christ, they sometimes directly and other times indirectly draw us to King Jesus and life in Him. Early in Israel's story, Moses anticipated their desire for a king when they reached the promised land. He stipulated in Deuteronomy 17:14–20 that the king not be self-indulgent and that "he shall write for himself in a book a copy of this law…and he shall read in it all the days of his life, that he may learn to fear the Lord his God by keeping all the words of this law and these statutes, and doing them, that his heart may not be lifted up above his brothers." Only a law keeper is a true king, making Jesus the Law Keeper, King of kings.

By Moses' standard, some of Israel's kings are good; most are bad. Samuel warned Israel before anointing their first king that when a king is set above them, he would become self-serving and self-aggrandizing (1 Sm 8:10–18)—just the opposite of the true king, Jesus, who "came not to be served, but to serve and give his life as a ransom for many" (Mk 10:45) Indeed, after God's people divide into two nations, each of the nation of Israel's nineteen kings, from Jeroboam to Hoshea, are deemed bad, "doing evil in the sight of the Lord." And of the nation of Judah's twenty kings, only seven are deemed good, "doing right in the eyes of the Lord." Josiah was one of those kings. He "walked in all the ways of David his father, he did not turn aside to the right or to the left" (2 Kgs 22:2). His reign foretells of Jesus in that he brought repair to the temple of God (22:3–7) and reforms the people of God in the goodness of the Law (2 Kgs 23). So this messianic description is his epitaph:

> Before him (Josiah) there was no king like him, who turned to the Lord with all his heart and with all his soul and with all his might, according to all the Law of Moses, nor did any like him arise after him. (2 Kgs 23:25)

The kings of Israel and Judah show the need for the messianic King who, as Emmanuel, "God with us," would bring nothing less than the full reign of God on earth. Psalm 72 is a prayer for this Royal Son and His reign on earth. Read in Christ, it is a prayer for Jesus' present and future reign, and the believer's reign in Him. It is helpful to quote it at length because it leads us into the next sections of Jesus' reign.

> Give the king your justice, O God, and your righteousness to the royal son! May he judge your people with righteousness, and your poor with justice!... May he defend the cause of the poor of the people, give deliverance to the children of the needy, and crush the oppressor! May they fear you while the sun endures, and as long as the moon, throughout all generations... In his days may the righteous flourish, and peace abound, till the moon be no more! May he have dominion from sea to sea, and from the River to the ends of the earth!... May all kings fall down before him, all nations serve him! For he delivers the needy when he calls, the poor and him who has no helper. He has pity on the weak and the needy, and saves the lives of the needy. From oppression and violence he redeems their life, and precious is their blood in his sight. Long may he live; may gold of Sheba be given to him! May prayer be

made for him continually and blessings invoked for him all the day! May there be abundance of grain in the land; on the tops of the mountains may it wave; may its fruit be like Lebanon; and may people blossom in the cities like the grass of the field! May his name endure forever, his fame continue as long as the sun! May people be blessed in him, all nations call him blessed! Blessed be the Lord, the God of Israel, who alone does wondrous things. Blessed be his glorious name forever; may the whole earth be filled with his glory! Amen and Amen! (Ps 72)

CHAPTER 10

Reign: Growth and Development

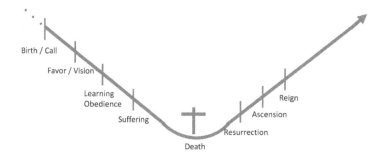

The Growth and Development of Jesus' Reign

Psalm 72 ends with this prayer for the messianic King's shalom reign:

> May the whole earth be filled with his glory.

Two thousand years after His death and glorification, we rejoice in how God Almighty is answering that prayer! The earth is filling with the glory of the King. Jesus anticipated this growth of His reign. Just prior to His crucifixion, He stated,

> This gospel of the kingdom will be proclaimed throughout the whole world as a testimony to all nations, and then the end will come. (Mt 24:14)

Earlier in His ministry, Jesus taught the growth of His reign through parables.

> What is the kingdom of God like? And to what shall I compare it? It is like a grain of mustard seed that a man took and sowed in his garden, and it grew and became a tree, and the birds of the air made nests in its branches. To what shall I compare the kingdom of God? It is like leaven that a woman took and hid in three measures of flour, until it was all leavened. (Luke 13:18–21)

Jesus' solitary life is that mustard seed that "fell into the earth and died" (Jn 12:24) so that the tree of the kingdom could rise and grow. His reign in this world is the leaven, invisible, yet filling the whole loaf. In Matthew 16:18, Jesus declared that He would build His church, and the gates of hell would not prevail against it. The gospel of the kingdom is a power that binds Satan (Rv 20:2) for this present age of Jesus' reign. And so the growth of His reign is a fact of history.

Philip Jenkins, in his book *The Next Christendom—the Coming of Global Christianity*, numerically chronicles this kingdom growth. Citing the work of his book, Charles Colson stated in 2011,

> Today Christianity is growing explosively outside of the West. For instance, in 1900 there were approximately 10 million Christians in Africa. By 2000, there were 360 million. By 2025, conservative estimates see the number rising to over 600 million. Those same estimates put the number of Christians in Latin America in 2025 at 640 million and in Asia at 460 million. (*CBN Online Magazine*, https://www1.cbn.com/how-christianity-growing-around-world)

Since formally inaugurating the kingdom of God with His solitary life, there are today more than 2.5 billion people who declare themselves Christians—over one-third of the world's population! Certainly a good measure of this number are merely nominal Christians, but many, many are actively living by His Spirit under the reign of Jesus. And that number continues to increase! In Jesus, people are entering the rule of God in dramatic numbers today!

Along with entering the kingdom, those under Jesus' reign—like their Master Himself—manifest signs of the kingdom in the work they do. These signs point to the nature of God's kingdom and bring glory to the King. As sung in "Joy to the World,"

> He comes to make His blessings flow far as the curse is found

or in Isaac Watt's hymn, "Jesus Shall Reign,"

> Blessings abound wherever He reigns;
> the prisoner leaps to lose his chains.
> The weary find eternal rest
> and all the sons of want are blessed!

Here is a statement from historian Paul Maier summarizing some of the "abounding blessings" of Jesus' reign on earth:

> Not only countless individual lives but civilization itself was transformed by Jesus Christ. In the ancient world, his teachings elevated brutish standards of morality, halted infanticide, enhanced human life, emancipated women, abolished slavery, inspired charities and relief organizations, created hospitals, established orphanages and founded schools. In medieval times, Christians almost single-handedly kept classical culture alive through recopying manuscripts, building libraries, moderating warfare through truce days, and

providing dispute arbitration. It was Christians who invented colleges and universities, dignified labor as a divine vocation, and extended the light of civilization to barbarians on the frontiers. In the modern era, Christian teaching, properly expressed, advanced science, instilled concepts of political and social and economic freedom, fostered justice, and provided the greatest single source of inspiration for the magnificent achievements in art, architecture, music, and literature that we treasure to the present day. (From David Feddes' paper, "The World-Changer," April 14, 2002)

Why are Christians involved in these good works? It's because they are under the reign of Jesus, anointed by His Spirit, with visions of His kingdom toward which they serve. Christians build hospitals because there is coming a new earth with no more mourning or crying or pain (Rv 21:4). In God's kingdom, there is health and shalom—wholeness—of which Scripture gives numerous glimpses. Hence, a Christian, Florence Nightingale, pioneered modern nursing, and another Christian, Henry Dunant, started the International Red Cross. Christian mission develops alphabets, teaches literacy, and begins universities because one day, "the earth will be filled with the knowledge of the glory of God as the waters cover the sea" (Hb 2:14). In that vision, the first book that the Christian Johannes Gutenberg printed upon inventing the printing press was a Bible. Christians labor for human dignity and freedoms because one day, "they shall sit every man under his vine and under his fig tree and no one shall make them afraid" (Mi 4:4). Thus, the archbishop of Canterbury was a major influence in drafting the Magna Carta. Christians moderate warfare and provide dispute arbitration because in the kingdom of God, "the wolf will lie down with the lamb" (Is 11:6) and "nations shall beat their swords into plowshares" (Is 2:4). Christians pursue beauty in the arts because in the New Jerusalem, the "glory of God gives the city its light," and "by its light the nations walk, and the kings of the earth will bring their glory into it" (Rv 21:24–25). Hence, Johann Sebastian Bach, when satisfied with the composition of a piece of music, would inscribe the letters "SDG" at the bottom of the page—*Soli Deo Gloria*, "for the glory of God alone"—his compositions then being nothing less than the yeast of Jesus' reign, bringing the beauty of God's kingdom into the dough of this world.

In 1994, D. James Kennedy and Jerry Newcombe wrote the book *What If Jesus Had Never Been Born*. It, too, details all the fruit of Jesus' reign through His followers in the areas of civilization, human dignity, works of mercy, education, civil liberties, health, arts, and music. Of particular significance is their chapter on science, "Thinking God's Thoughts after Him." It helps us to recognize even more of the yeast of Jesus' reign in our world today. In the last two hundred years, science has contributed much to the well-being of our world, reflecting the goodness of God's kingdom. In that chapter, Kennedy and Newcombe list thirty branches of science founded by Bible-believing, Spirit-anointed servants of the King of kings. Some samples are bacteriology by Louis Pasteur, calculus by Isaac Newton, celestial mechanics by Johannes Kepler, chemistry by Robert Boyle, computer science by Charles Babbage, genetics by Gregor Mendel, hydrostatics by Blaise Pascal. As Dinesh D'Souza states in his 2007 book *What's so Great About Christianity*,

> An unbiased look at the history of science shows that modern science is an invention of medieval Christianity; and that the greatest breakthroughs in scientific reason have largely been the work of Christians... Where did Western man get his faith in a unified, ordered and accessible universe? How did we go from chaos to cosmos? My answer, in a word, Christianity... Christianity reinvigorated the idea of an ordered cosmos by envisioning the universe as following laws that embody the rationality of God the creator. (pp 84, 93)

Through science, reason, and technology, our world today is becoming increasingly healthy and wealthy, safer and better educated—all inklings of the kingdom. Hunger is vanishing—undernourished people in the world fell from 19 percent in 1990 to 10.8 percent in 2018; the United Nations has set a goal of zero hunger by 2030 (https://www.undp.org/content/undp/en/home/sustainable-development-goals/goal-2-zero-hunger.html).

People are living longer—on average now 71.5 years, up six years since 1990. Wealth is growing—in the 1950s, a majority of humanity had always lived in extreme poverty (less than two dollars per day); in the 1980s, 44 percent; today, less than 10 percent. Literacy and learning are increasing—in 1970, three-fourths of the world was illiterate; today, four-fifths can read. The increasing safety of the world is described by Harvard professor Steven Pinker in his book *The Better Angels of our Nature*. Summarizing his research, Pinker states in its introduction,

> This book is about what may be the most important thing that has ever happened in human history. Believe it or not violence has declined over long stretches of time, and today we may be living in the most peaceable era of our species' existence. Violence has declined by dramatic degrees all over the world in many spheres of behavior: genocide, war, human sacrifice, torture, slavery, and the treatment of racial minorities, women, children, and animals.

The daily news notwithstanding, the world continues to grow as a safer place—and more abundant! Nourishing exotic food from around the world graces more and more dining tables day by day, signs of the messianic banquet (Is 25:6, Luke 14:15). In this same vein, we recognize many "kingdom progresses" in our age of the earth. In a January 5, 2019, *New York Times* article titled "Why 2018 Was the Best Year Ever," Nicholas Kristoff adds this: "Each day on average 295,000 people gain access to electricity for the first time;

305,000 access clean drinking water for the first time; and 620,000 people are able to get online for the first time." Such blessing contributes to human flourishing.

The prophet Isaiah declares of the messianic King,

> And of the increase of his government and of
> peace there will be no end. (Is 9:7)

"The kingdom of this world has become the Kingdom of our God and of His Christ, and He shall reign forever and ever" (Rv 11:15). The Messiah's reign will grow in this world.

> The Lord says to my Lord: "Sit at my right hand,
> until I make your enemies your footstool." (Ps
> 110:1)

We are seeing this in the number of people entering His kingdom in personal allegiance to the King. We are seeing this also in the fruit of His reign through His followers in this world, both directly and indirectly. That fruit can be understood as signs of the kingdom, the yeast of His reign. Is hunger one of the enemies being put under Jesus' feet? Illiteracy? Sickness? Violence? Ignorance? Oppression? When Jesus walked the earth, He certainly treated those forces as alien powers, even while bringing the kingdom's health and wholeness to others and drawing people to Himself as King. In 1 Corinthians 15, the apostle Paul, drawing from Psalms 110 and 2, confirms Jesus' growing reign in this age of the earth. At the end of this age, Paul writes in verse 24, Jesus will deliver His kingdom to God the Father *after* "destroying every rule and every authority and every power. For he must reign until he has put all his enemies under his feet. The last enemy to be destroyed is death. For God has put all things in subjection under his feet" (vv. 25–27).

Therefore, Christians not only rejoice in the growing numbers of people entering the kingdom through personal allegiance to the King. We also rejoice in the rising yeast of His reign in signs of the kingdom, the new earth to come. The kingdom is more than an individual relationship with the King. Yes, that is its entry point, but the kingdom is also social and political and cultural. God made this clear in the old covenant by calling a nation, Israel, into being and giving it laws and culture. That nation was a forerunner of the future kingdom society, the New Jerusalem. Jesus fulfilled Israel's calling, and now His Spirit continues to empower both His servants, the church, and our world with kingdom vision and works toward that vision. So Christians view human "progress" in the light of this kingdom, glorifying Jesus as the King of kings, calling people to Him as Lord, and working in the power of His Spirit to manifest signs of that kingdom which is and is to come.

CHAPTER 11

Reign: Opposition and Triumph

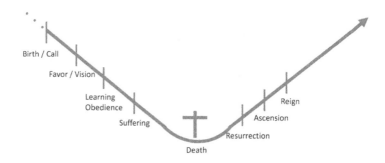

Opposition to Jesus' Reign

Paradoxically, in the very same Matthew 24 passage that Jesus foretells the growth of the gospel of His kingdom throughout the whole world (v. 14), He also teaches that "lawlessness will increase" in the course of this age (v. 12). He makes this clear too in His parable of the wheat and tares in Matthew 13:24–30.

> Let both [good seeds and weeds] grow together
> until the harvest. (Mt 13:30)

In further explanation, Jesus adds,

> The one who sows the good seed is the Son of
> Man. The field is the world, and the good seed is
> the sons of the kingdom. The weeds are the sons
> of the evil one, and the enemy who sowed them
> is the devil. The harvest is the end of the age, and
> the reapers are angels. Just as the weeds are gath-
> ered and burned with fire, so will it be at the end
> of the age. (Mt 13:38–41)

The apostle Paul confirms this increase in lawlessness in 2
Timothy 3:1–5:

> But understand this, that in the last days there
> will come times of difficulty. For people will be
> lovers of self, lovers of money, proud, arrogant,
> abusive, disobedient to their parents, ungrate-
> ful, unholy, heartless, unappeasable, slanderous,
> without self-control, brutal, not loving good,
> treacherous reckless, swollen with conceit, lovers
> of pleasure rather than lovers of God, having the
> appearance of godliness but denying its power.

Even as the kingdom grows and develops in this age of Jesus'
reign, so, too, will the spirit of godlessness and lawlessness increase!
This paradox can be understood using the analogy of a newborn
who, while yet an infant, contracts a slow-growing cancer. A baby
does not remain an infant. It grows, develops, and matures toward
adulthood. This development is good and healthy. Such is the growth
of Jesus' reign, the Seed of new life in this world. Yet even as this
child is maturing, the cancer, too, develops and "matures." This is
the spirit of lawlessness, opposition to the reign of Christ, godlessness. Like a cancer, sin is parasitical. Even as goodness grows, anti-
goodness grows. Both life and death, Christ and godlessness, are at
work in this age (the child). (And the cancer would completely end

the life of the child/world, save the promised victory of Jesus.) The internet, for example, creates increasing good and increasing evil. So this increase of godlessness is best understood in various dimensions of effect. Along with the extent of lawlessness, it also refers to the social pressure of lawlessness. Its presence will be more pervasive; its pressure will increase. Along with the immorality of lawlessness, it also refers to the spirit of human self-exaltation in the denial of God. Godless human pride will increase and "mature." In various ways then, through the course of this age, Jesus teaches that "lawlessness" will increase, opposition to His reign—opposition that will encroach on freedoms for the followers of Jesus (Mt 24:9).

The scriptural witness to this spirit of godlessness goes all the way back to the garden of Eden when Satan tempted mankind to forsake God's law and eat of the tree of the knowledge of good and evil:

> For when you eat of it your eyes will be opened,
> and you will be like God, knowing good and evil.
> (Gn 3:5)

Lawlessness inevitably leads to the exaltation of man as God, humanity itself determining right and wrong. It is the spirit of the Antichrist, Jesus Christ being the Law-Abiding, Lawful One. This increase in godlessness was foretold in the story of the Tower of Babel. There, mankind, while yet speaking only one language, organized themselves to "build a city and a tower with its top in the heavens, and *'let us make a name for ourselves,'* lest we be dispersed over the face of the whole earth" (Gn 11:4; emphasis mine). Here is human arrogance, self-exaltation, and disobedience to God's command to fill the earth and subdue it. This early, Babel foretells the coming of another "Babel"—Babylon, a proud and mighty nation which opposed God's people in the Old Covenant (linguistically, Babel and Babylon are related words). Together, they anticipate the final Babylon of Revelation 17–18. Babylon represents human arrogance, worldly achievement, and human glory apart from God. It is personified in King Nebuchadnezzar of Babylon, who, before being humbled by God, declared,

> Is not this great Babylon, which I have built by
> my mighty power as a royal residence and for the
> glory of my majesty? (Dn 4:30)

It is the human embodiment of the Satanic spirit described in Isaiah 14:13–14 who said in his heart,

> I will ascend to heaven above the stars of God, I
> will set my throne on high... I will ascend above
> the heights of the clouds; I will make myself like
> the Most High. (Is 14:13–14)

But just as He did with the Tower of Babel, God judged Nebuchadnezzar for such audacity and self-exaltation, mercifully humbling him into a beast of the field until he could eventually confess in true sanity:

> Blessed be the Most High. I praise and honor
> him who lives forever, for his dominion is an
> everlasting dominion, and his kingdom endures
> from generation to generation. (4:34)

The heart of salvation is this reversal toward true sanity!

However, in the case of Satan's pride and self-exaltation, God did not choose to show such mercy. In Satan's story, God's justice is glorified.

> But you are brought down to Sheol, to the far
> reaches of the pit... Your pomp is brought down
> to Sheol, the sound of your harps; maggots are
> laid as a bed beneath you, and worms are your
> covers. How you are fallen from heaven, O Day
> Star, son of Dawn! (Is 14:15, 11–12)

This judgment of Satan is similar to the judgment of the ultimate human Babylon described in Revelation 18. There is no mercy in this act of judgment; it is a final judgment of human self-glorification, an affirmation of the justice of God.

> Fallen, fallen is Babylon the great! She has become a dwelling place for demons, a haunt for every unclean spirit… For all nations have drunk the wine of the passion of her sexual immorality, and the kings of the earth have committed immorality with her, and the merchants of the earth have grown rich from the power of her luxurious living… Alas! Alas! You great city, you mighty city, Babylon! For in a single hour your judgment has come. (Rv 18:2–3, 10)

Undoubtedly, the original readers of the book of Revelation would have understood this Babylon to be the city of Rome, the center of the godless Roman empire. And when Rome fell in AD 375, it was certainly a measure of the fulfillment of this Word. It was a judgment of God against the human pride and self-exaltation of Rome. But it was not the *final judgment* against the "Babel/ Babylonian manifestation." (And as such, that judgment bore within it mercy for the people of God as all God's judgments do prior to the Ultimate Judgment—see next chapter.)

The final Babylon is still growing in this world—the increasing spirit of lawlessness (Mt 24:12), the increasing spirit of "making a name for ourselves" (Gn 11:4), "humanism." This is also the spirit of the "anti-Christ" or "lawless one." The apostolic teaching makes evident that this spirit is both present in our age today and will eventually manifest itself in an individual human Antichrist.

> Children, it is the last hour, and as you have heard that antichrist is coming, so now many antichrists have come… Every spirit that does not confess Jesus is not from God. This is the spirit of the antichrist, which you heard was coming and now is in the world already. (1 Jn 2:18, 4:3)

The apostle Paul amplifies this in 2 Thessalonians 2. Prior to the day of the return of the Lord Jesus Christ and the believer's reunion with Him,

> The rebellion comes first, and the man of law-
> lessness is revealed, the son of destruction, who
> opposes and exalts himself against every so-called
> god or object of worship, so that he takes his seat
> in the temple of God, proclaiming himself to be
> God. (2 Thes 2:3–4)

Clearly, Paul has here in mind an individual lawless person, the Antichrist. But later in this chapter, he also makes clear that this individual is just the climactic manifestation of a growing spirit of lawlessness. In verses 7–12, Paul describes this as the "mystery of lawlessness" which is being restrained in our age by the Spirit of God. This restraining work of the Spirit will one day draw back (v. 7), opening the way for the "lawless one to be revealed, who the Lord Jesus will kill with the breath of his mouth and bring to nothing by the appearance of his coming" (v. 8). This withdrawal of the Spirit leading to the increase of lawlessness and the manifestation of the Antichrist will divide humanity.

> The coming of the lawless one is by the activ-
> ity of Satan with all power and false signs and
> wonders, and with all wicked deception for those
> who are perishing, because they refused to love
> the truth and so be saved. (2 Thes 2:9–10)

The "mystery of lawlessness" in our day is not difficult to see. Lawless definitions of gender and marriage have taken hold in Western society, definitions which oppose both the laws of nature and revealed laws of God in Scripture. Is gender only a social construct? Is marriage only a contract between any two people who feel in love with each other? Is family just any group of people who care for each other? The spirit of lawlessness, too, is manifest in the abortion and euthanasia debates. Will life be defined according to economic value or God's laws in nature and Scripture? Are human rights determined by personal convenience or social productivity alone?

The power to increase lawlessness too is evident in the developments of technology. Through technology, pressure is exerted on people to abide by laws that are contrary to God's will. For example, the Chinese government today has begun to give its citizens a "social credit rating," akin to a financial credit rating common in Western society. The social credit rating will help to align its citizens with its governmental values. Social media posts, financial transactions, every movement and activity of its citizens contribute to their social credit rating which, in turn, opens or closes doors of opportunity in that society. It is easy to envision this happening in more and more societies or, eventually, on a grand scale in a globally unified society. In these types of developments, the powers of lawlessness will put pressure on the people of God who give first allegiance to His laws in honor to their King, Jesus Christ.

Jesus foretold this increasing opposition to His reign and the pressure that it would exert on His followers.

> They will deliver you up to tribulation and put you to death, and you will be hated by all nations for my name's sake. And then many will fall away and betray one another and hate one another. And many false prophets will arise and lead many astray. And because lawlessness will be increased, the love of many will grow cold. (Mt 24:9–12)

Then Jesus added,

> But the one who endures to the end will be saved.

Will you endure in an age of increasing lawlessness when evil makes its "last stand"? The key to godly endurance is living deeply, through faith and repentance, in the plotline of Jesus' life and the promise of the eventual triumph of His reign.

The Triumph of Jesus' Reign

The growing reign of Jesus in our age and the increasing lawlessness also within it is a paradox which brings stress on earth. This is Jesus' teaching in Matthew 24. It is stress not only against His followers; it is global stress—socially, religiously, and physically.

> You will hear of wars and rumors of wars. (Mt 24:6)

> There will be famines and earthquakes in various places. (Mt 24:7)

> False Christs and false prophets will arise and perform great signs and wonders, so as to lead astray, if possible, even the elect. (Mt 24:24)

> After the tribulation of those days the sun will be darkened and the moon will not give its light, and the stars will fall from heaven, and the powers of heavens will be shaken. (Mt 24:29)

The analogy that Jesus uses to explain this stress is pregnancy and labor, birth pains leading to the triumphant delivery of new life. Referring to wars and famines and earthquakes, Jesus comments:

> All these are but the beginning of the birth pains. (Mt 24:8)

In Jesus' understanding, the impact of His ministry was to impregnate this world with His kingdom, its future—just as a mother becomes pregnant with her future generation. Jesus Himself is the seed of eternal life who has inseminated this age with its future kingdom. In this sense, Jesus did not come to bring His people out of the world to heaven; He came to bring heaven on earth, into this world. In John 12:24–25, He refers to His life as that inseminating seed. Alluding to His forthcoming death, He states:

> Truly, truly, I say to you, unless a grain of wheat falls into the earth and dies, it remains alone; but if it dies, it bears much fruit. Whoever loves his life loses it and whoever hates his life in this world will keep it for eternal life. (Jn 12:24–25)

Because Jesus came and died, our world is now pregnant with its future. That is how Christians understand the kingdom in relation to the age we now live in. Jesus' kingdom is in this world, like new life in a mother's womb, new life that is growing and growing! This analogy also gives perspective on the organic relationship between the present age and the one to come. Yes, the new earth will be "new," but it will have natural ties with this present age, like a mother and child.

Like human birth, however, that new life comes forth out of the womb only with the stress and pain of delivery. When that stress reaches its highest point of tribulation, then comes "delivery"—the birth of the new earth. This birth is in conjunction with Jesus' glorious return. In Matthew 24:29–31, Jesus describes that delivery:

> The powers of heaven will be shaken. Then will appear in heaven the sign of the Son of Man, and then all the tribes of the earth will mourn, and they will see the Son of Man coming on the clouds of heaven with power and great glory. And he will send out his angels with a loud trumpet call, and they will gather his elect from the four winds, from one end of heaven to the other.

This is the triumph of the reign of Jesus. It is the safe delivery of His kingdom from the womb of this world, with its perils of lawlessness, to become the *new heaven and earth*.

Pregnancy and birth then is one paradigm and predictor of the course of Jesus' kingdom in this age. An even more significant paradigm and predictor is the story (plotline) of Jesus' own life—His ministry, suffering, death, and resurrection. All three synoptic gospels place Jesus' teaching on the course of this age, the signs of its coming to an end, and the promise of His triumphant return just prior to their passion narratives (Mt 24, Mk 13, Luke 21). These chapters closely resemble each other. In each, Jesus describes the growing stress of this age, the growing persecution of His followers—with its warning lest their "love grows cold," the growing proclamation of the gospel of the kingdom, the rise of false prophets, the growing physical convulsions of earth, all leading to His triumphant return in glory. He then concludes His teaching about these signs of the future with a call to "be alert," "stay awake," "pray and watch" (Mk 13:37, Luke 21:36). He also makes this most important statement:

> Truly, I say to you, this generation will not pass away until all these things take place. Heaven and earth will pass away, but my words will not pass away. (Mk 13:30–31, Mt 24:34–35, Luke 21:32–33)

With that statement, Jesus is declaring that His immediate generation will see the future of this age happen right before their very eyes!

> This generation will not pass away until all these things take place.

He himself is going to portray the future of this age of the earth with His own life, sufferings, and death—and resurrection. His kingdom ministry has now reached a fullness whereby He personally will go through the events of the future. He will be "hated by all nations" and "delivered up to tribulation" (Mt 24:9). He will be "delivered over to councils," "beaten," and "made to stand before governors and kings" (Mk 13:9)—as He was before Pilate and Herod. He will be "brought to trial" and "delivered over" (Mk 13:11). He will see "lawlessness increase" (Mt 24:12)—even as the religious and political leaders conspire to do Him injustice. He will experience the love of His followers "grow cold" (Mt 24:12) and see the "many who fall away and betray one another" (Mt 24:10)—as His disciples Peter and Judas will do. Despite asking them to "watch and pray and stay alert" in the garden of Gethsemane, His disciples fall asleep (Mt 26:36–46), overwhelmed by the stress of the hour.

Yet through all this, Jesus remains faithful in obedience. He heeds His own admonition in Matthew 24:13:

He who endures to the end will be saved.

Jesus remains obedient in suffering in order to become the messianic Savior, the One who will not only die to atone for the sins of His people but also be the One who, by His Spirit, guides His people in their faithfulness through to the end of the age. He will ensure the salvation of His elect by His own faithfulness.

Beyond injustice, imprisonment, and beatings, Jesus also foretold that some of His followers would be put to death (Luke 21:16). Jesus is crucified. And when He died, the earth shook (Mt 27:51) and the sun turned black and darkness covered the land (Mt 27:45—cf. 24:29). Indeed, that generation saw the future of our age enacted before their very eyes—even its geological convulsions of labor! Seeing this faithfulness of their Messiah will inspire all future generations of the godly in their obedience to God.

But Jesus' story does not end in death.

The one who endures to the end will be saved.

He endured and was saved. Beyond death, Jesus is resurrected to new life. His resurrection thus foretells His "coming again in clouds with great power and glory." Even when it may appear that God's kingdom in this age has met its end, Jesus will return to intervene and ensure the safe delivery of the godly and the continuance of His kingdom! The promise of Jesus' triumphant return is tied directly to His resurrection.

The future has already happened! Jesus' life, death, and resurrection are the central events of history. His plotline was foretold in the Old Testament and displayed in His person which now foretells the course of His kingdom in the developments of this age. In Him, a new kingdom has been conceived and is growing in the womb of this age. That new kingdom is the future of our world and universe, the new earth and heaven. But that kingdom will be tried and tested as this age draws to its close, even to the point of wondering whether it will carry the day. Fear not, Jesus will return to ensure the safe delivery of His kingdom from the womb of this world. His resurrection guarantees it!

CHAPTER 12

Return and Final Judgment

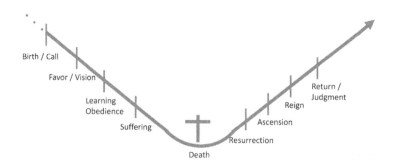

Birth / Call

Favor / Vision

Learning
Obedience

Suffering

Death

Resurrection

Ascension

Reign

Return /
Judgment

The nature of Jesus' second coming stands in stark contrast with His first coming. His birth in Bethlehem was marked by humility, the babe placed in a manger in a stable. It was a relatively private event, in quietness and darkness of night, in a small Middle Eastern town. Indeed, in His first coming, Jesus' entrance was like that inseminating seed entering the quietness and darkness of a womb. His return, however, will be public, dramatic, and glorious—a birth of the new age to come!

At His ascension, His disciples were told,

> This Jesus, who was taken up from you into heaven, will come in the same way you saw him go into heaven. (Acts 1:10)

Jesus Himself foretold His return with these words:

> At that time, the sign of the Son of Man will
> appear in the sky, and all the nations of the earth
> will mourn. They will see the Son of Man com-
> ing on the clouds of the sky, with power and great
> glory. (Mt 24:30)

Revelation 1:7 adds,

> Behold, he is coming with the clouds, and every
> eye will see him, even those who pierced him, and
> all tribes of the earth will wail on account of him.

The apostle Paul describes Jesus' triumphant return like an
alarm clock awakening all creation, summoning mankind before His
presence:

> For the Lord himself will descend from heaven with
> a cry of command, with the voice of an archangel,
> and with the sound of the trumpet of God. And the
> dead in Christ will rise first. Then we who are alive,
> who are left, will be caught up together with them
> in the clouds to meet the Lord in the air, and so we
> will always be with the Lord. (1 Thes 4:16–17)

This public awakening is a summons that those who are in
Christ have longed for, having lived in anticipation of and preparation for this Day of the Lord. Hence, upon awakening, they gather
up to meet Him in the clouds and welcome His return to our world,
like children running out to meet their dad upon his return home
from work. Jesus' people are not "raptured" out of this world. No, the
King of this world is coming home. Or to use a more exact analogy,
one common to the day of Paul's writing, the rapture is the event of
the citizens of God's kingdom coming out of the city to welcome
their triumphant Commander and His armies back home in victo-

rious procession. In Roman military protocol, upon their return to the city of Rome, the triumphant military and its captives would first camp outside of the city. Then a messenger would be sent into the city Senate to inform them of the military's return.

The Senate would, in turn, ask the city planners to prepare for their formal return, preparation which included the erection of an Arch of Triumph and making fragrant the city streets. Once preparations had concluded, a signal was made via trumpet blast whereupon the citizens of Rome would themselves gather outside the city with the military to then march back into their home city with the commander, the military, and the captives in triumphant procession. It is in this sense then that Christians are "caught up together" with the Lord Jesus Christ to usher him home—in order to conclude the work of His victorious reign in this age and lead us into the age to come.

That concluding, climactic work of King Jesus in this age of our world is to subject it to final judgment. It is the culmination and consummation of our age, and the reality of judgment provides it moral meaning.

> God has fixed a day in which He will judge the world in righteousness by a man whom He has appointed; and of this he has given assurance to all by raising him from the dead. (Acts 17:31)

Jesus foretold His work of judgment in John 5:22–23:

> The Father judges no one, but has given all judgment to the Son, that all may honor the Son, just as they honor the Father. Whoever does not honor the Son does not honor the Father who sent him.

The apostle Paul confirms this in his teaching:

> For we must all appear before the judgment seat of Christ, so that each one may receive what is

due for what he has done in the body, whether
good or evil. (2 Cor 5:10)

Paul, too, understands that this Day of Final Judgment will
occur upon Jesus' return, His "appearing":

> I have finished the race, I have kept the faith.
> Henceforth there is laid up for me the crown
> of righteousness, which the Lord, the righteous
> judge, will award to me on that Day, and not
> only to me but also to all who have loved his
> appearing. (2 Tm 4:7–8)

Again,

> For the grace of God has appeared, bringing
> salvation for all people, training us to renounce
> ungodliness and worldly passions, and to live
> self-controlled, upright, and godly lives in the
> present age, waiting for our blessed hope, the
> appearing of the glory of our great God and
> Savior Jesus Christ. (Ti 2:11–13)

It is the reality of our final judgment upon Jesus' return that
provides vision and impetus to "renounce ungodliness and worldly
passions" and live "godly lives in this present age."

The Day of the Lord

In the larger context of Scripture, this "appearing of the glory
of our great God and Savior Jesus Christ" is known as the Day of the
Lord. It is a day of both judgment and salvation. It is a day that the
prophets of the Old Testament regularly speak of.

> Behold, the day of the Lord comes, cruel, with
> wrath and fierce anger, to make the land a deso-
> lation and to destroy its sinners from it. (Is 13:9)

As Jesus Himself taught, it is a day that will come suddenly, and people will be unprepared for it (cf. Mt 24:36–51). The prophet Zephaniah proclaims,

> The great day of the Lord is near, near and has-
> tening fast; the sound of the day of the Lord is
> bitter; the mighty man cries aloud there... In the
> fire of God's jealousy, all the earth shall be con-
> sumed for a full and sudden end he will make of
> all the inhabitants of earth. (Zep 1:14, 18)

This Day of the Lord contains both judgment against sin and salvation for the people of God.

> Let the nations stir themselves up and come up
> to the Valley of Jehoshaphat; for there I will sit
> to judge all the surrounding nations. Put in the
> sickle for the harvest is ripe... The Lord roars
> from Zion and utters his voice from Jerusalem
> and the heavens and the earth quake. But the
> Lord is a refuge to his people, a stronghold to
> the people of Israel. So you shall know that I
> am the Lord your God, who dwells in Zion, my
> holy mountain. And Jerusalem shall be holy, and
> strangers shall never again pass through it. And
> in that day the mountains shall drip sweet wine,
> and the hills shall flow with milk, and all the
> streambeds of Judah shall flow with water; and a
> fountain shall come forth from the house of the
> Lord and water from the Valley of Shittim. (Jl
> 3:12–13, 16–18)

This final Day of the Lord will bring creation's story in this age to its close and usher in the *new heaven and earth*. It is a straightforward connection from Joel's words above to the apostle John's vision of the New Jerusalem at the end of Revelation:

> Nothing unclean will ever enter it, not anyone who does what is detestable or false. (Rv 21:26)

> Then the angel showed me the river of the water of life, bright as crystal, flowing from the throne of God and of the Lamb through the middle of the street of the city. (Rv 22:1–2)

The New Jerusalem shall be holy, a place of union between God and His people, nourished by the waters of the Spirit.

Final Judgment Prefigured

Jesus' return constitutes the *ultimate* Day of the Lord, bringing both judgment and salvation. Reading Scripture in Christ, however, we see numerous "Days of the Lord," each bringing judgment and salvation, each prefiguring a central revelatory fulfillment in Jesus' death as God's "Day" of both judgment and salvation, each preparing God's people for the final Day of the Lord in the consummation of our age.

The Day of the Lord came as a flood in Noah's day.

> The Lord saw that the wickedness of man was great in the earth… So the Lord said, "I will blot out man whom I have created from the face of the land…for I am sorry that I have made them. But Noah found favor in the eyes of the Lord. (Gn 6:5–8)

Thus, the Day came, bringing both judgment against wickedness and salvation to Noah and his family, they who lived in obedience to God's Word, putting their lives and trust in the ark of wood (the ark being a type of Jesus/the cross). Jesus himself likened the flood event to His coming again:

> As in the days of Noah, so will be the coming of the Son of Man. For as in those days before the flood they were eating and drinking, marrying and giving in marriage, until the day when Noah entered the ark, and they were unaware until the flood came and swept them all away, so will be the coming of the Son of Man. Then two men will be in the field; one will be taken and one left. Two women will be grinding at the mill; one will be taken and one left. Therefore, stay awake, for you do not know on what day your Lord is coming. (Mt 24:37–42)

Do note from this passage that those who are taken away from the earth are the unprepared godless, not the godly (in some sort of "rapture")—just as in Noah's day, the wicked are swept away! "Blessed are the meek, they shall inherit the earth" (Mt 5:5).

Another Day of the Lord in the Old Testament involves Israel's deliverance from Egypt. There, God sent judgment against proud Pharaoh and in those acts of judgment (Ex 7–13), salvation, too, comes. God's people are set free. After the tenth and final plague, the death of the firstborn of Egypt, Pharaoh cries,

> Up, go out from among my people, both you and the people of Israel; and go, serve the Lord, as you have said. Take your flocks and your herds, as you have said, and be gone. (Ex 12:31)

Freedom for the people of God—through the death of God's only begotten, firstborn Son—there prefigured!

The Day of the Lord, too, is prefigured in God's judgment against Israel itself, executed through the hand of Babylon. Jerusalem was destroyed and its people exiled because of their sins of idolatry and Sabbath breaking (Is 58, Jer 17:19–23), even the seventy-year length of their exile being tied to not giving the land its Sabbath rest (Lv 25:4, 2 Chr 36:21). Yet this judgment also brought salvation. Through it, God's people are humbled and purified. They return to God in repentance (Dn 9:1–19), and God does a work of restoration with them in their return, rebuilding the city and its temple.

Final Judgment Affirmed

In the same "Day of the Lord" event then come both judgment and salvation. In the Old Testament, these events are *prophetic* judgments, pointing to God's act of judgment and salvation in the death of Jesus Christ. His death is history's *central* judgment, a day of the Lord bringing punishment against sin and salvation for God's people. Jesus' death and resurrection, therefore, confirms the reality of a final judgment to come. There will be a Judgment Day because on the cross, Jesus was judged for sin's guilt. And that day will also bring salvation because Jesus' resurrection confirms that His death bore the full curse of sin for His people. Therefore, Jesus' death both warns and calls us to prepare for that ultimate Day of the Lord in His return, the day of punishment for sin and salvation for the people of God, the day of both God's justice and grace in Christ.

Although Jesus' death is God's central act of judgment and salvation, events in these "last days" (Acts 2:17, 1 Pt 4:7), our current time in this age, also represent significant acts of God's judgment. These acts of judgment are meant to *affirm* God's judgment of sin in Jesus' death and prepare us for the Day of His return.

In AD 70, Roman military might entered Jerusalem and destroyed its temple. Jesus foretold this event (Mt 24:1–2). The significance of this judgment was that it validated Jesus Himself as God's new covenant temple, the locale of God's presence on earth (cf. Jn 2:21). It also confirmed that Jesus had indeed fulfilled the Old Covenant temple structure system of sacrificial worship and has now begun the new covenant of life with God in Himself. In foretelling this destruction, Jesus also warned His followers to flee Jerusalem when it occurs, when the "abomination of desolation" stands in the holy place (Mt 24:15). This Word had a major fulfillment when Rome built a temple to Zeus on the site in which the former temple once stood and there offered a pig on its altar of sacrifice—complete sacrilege! Recognizing this abomination, Jesus' followers fled Judea and began to spread the gospel of His kingdom into the rest of the world. God's judgments always contain mercy and salvation for His people, furthering His kingdom advance in this age.

The book of Revelation also describes judgments of God in this age prior to Jesus' return. They are released through seals opening (Rv 6), trumpets blowing (Rv 8), and bowls being poured out (Rv 16). They bring stress on earth—war, famine, pestilence, plague, pain, and death. They are meant to warn mankind of the final Day of the Lord to come and lead them into repentance. Sadly,

> those who were not killed by these plagues did not repent of the works of their hands nor give up worshiping demons and idols of gold and silver and bronze and stone and wood, which cannot see or walk, nor did they repent of their murders or their sorceries or their sexual immorality or their thefts. (Rv 9:20–21)

Yet God preserves and sanctifies His people through the course of these judgments. They are the 144,000 who

> follow the Lamb wherever he goes. They have been redeemed from mankind as firstfruits for God and the Lamb, and in their mouth no lie was found, for they are blameless. (Rv 14:5)

In our day, does God yet send acts of judgment to warn people of the Day of Christ to come? Was 9/11 a judgment of God against America? Is COVID-19 a judgment of God against the whole globe? Can a child's rejection of Christ be a judgment of God against one's own lack of faith integrity? The Christian confirms this assessment, receiving them as events meant to awaken mankind and declare the righteousness of the Sovereign God, preparing us for the final judgment to come. Such events find meaning in the prophetic visions of the Revelation, and they lead us into self-searching and repentance. They humble and call us back to God, regrounding our lives in forgiveness through Christ, then furthering His work of salvation in our world. God's judgments in our day, as centered in the meaning of Jesus' death, whether they be personal, national, or global, always contain seeds of mercy and salvation for His people, building His kingdom on earth.

The Glory of Jesus as the Substance of Judgment

The simplest way to understand the nature of God's final judgment is as a universal manifestation of the glory of Jesus Christ, His person and work. As noted earlier, Jesus declared that judgment has been "given to Him" (Jn 5:22), and the apostolic teaching affirms that we must "all appear before the judgment seat of Christ" (2 Cor 5:10). Further, that future event is described in Titus 2:13 as "the appearing of the GLORY of our great God and Savior Jesus Christ." Therefore, the final judgment for each individual can be best understood in accord with the question, to what degree is the glory of Jesus Christ the faith, hope, and love of your life?

Descents of Glory

Reading Scripture in Christ, we recognize numerous descents of divine glory, all of which point toward Jesus' final descent, a descent that will bring His full and permanent glory on earth (Rv 21:3). In the Old Testament, that descent of glory is seen in the pillars of cloud and fire which protected and led the people of God in their exodus from Egypt (Ex 13:21–22). Later in that journey, after Moses had overseen the careful construction of the tabernacle, its furnishings, and the preparation of its priesthood, the glory of God descended upon that tent of meeting.

> And Moses was not able to enter the tent of meeting because the cloud settled on it, and the glory of the Lord filled the tabernacle. (Ex 40:35)

Thereupon, "the cloud of the Lord was on the tabernacle by day, and fire was in it by night" (v. 38). This is a significant development because now, the descent and presence of God's glory is connected to His tabernacle, the tent of meeting. This anticipates a similar descent when King Solomon, later in Israel's story, completes the construction of the temple building, patterned after the tabernacle, and replacing it. Upon Solomon's prayer of dedication for the temple,

> fire came down from heaven and consumed the burnt offerings and the sacrifices, and the glory of the Lord filled the temple. And the priests could not enter the house of the Lord, because the glory of the Lord filled the Lord's house. When all the people of Israel saw the fire come down and the glory of the Lord on the temple, they bowed down with their faces to the ground on the pavement and worshiped and gave thanks to the Lord, saying, "For he is good, for his steadfast love endures forever." (2 Chr 7:1–3)

What a picture this gives of Jesus' return when "every knee shall bow and every tongue confess that Jesus Christ is Lord" (Phil 2:10–11). On that occasion, there will be mourning (Rv 1:7), but there will also be thanksgiving for the people of God—those who have built faith, hope, and love toward that manifestation of His glory.

The significance of connecting the descent of God's glory upon His temple comes in seeing the bigger picture of the Bible. The creation story of Genesis 1 is most truly understood as the construction and dedication of a temple building, mankind placed in it on the sixth day as an image of the Creator (Gn 1:26), designated to exercise dominion over the earth—to serve and bless the Creator in their work. Thereafter, God rests in His creation, all creation thereby becoming a "tent of meeting" between God and mankind. Sin disrupted this relationship and alienated mankind and their Maker. But Jesus, the second Adam, has come to restore all creation again as

God's tent of meeting. This will happen upon His return in glory. Beyond the Day of Judgment, the new heaven and new earth will be creation restored as the temple of God:

> Behold, the dwelling place of God is with man.
> He will dwell with them, and they will be his
> people, and God himself will be with them as
> their God. (Rv 21:3)

This is the big story of the Bible, creation restored as the temple of God. It is in that context the Old Testament descents of God's glory upon the tabernacle and Solomon's temple must be understood. Solomon himself designed his temple to be representative of the original garden of Eden.

> Around all the walls of the house he carved
> engraved figures of cherubim and palm trees and
> open flowers, in the inner and outer rooms. (1
> Kgs 6:29)

So the big picture Bible story of the flow of God's "tent of meeting" is *creation*, then *tabernacle, temple*, Jesus, *Christ's body* (the church), then *creation restored*.

Toward that future Day, two other biblical descents of God's glory must be noted. The first is the incarnation.

> The Word became flesh and dwelt among us, and
> we have seen his glory, glory as of the only Son
> from the Father, full of grace and truth. (Jn 1:14)

The manifestation of God's glory in the person of Jesus fulfills the temple building as His place of meeting. We now meet with God through Jesus, in Spirit and truth (Jn 4:24). Jesus referred to Himself as the Temple (Jn 2:21), and His one sacrifice fulfilled for all time the purposes of the many sacrifices performed at the tent/building (Heb 10:12).

But God's personal descent in the glory of Jesus was only the means to a greater end—the formation of a new temple in this age prior to His return. That new covenant temple is the people of God, those in Christ.

> Christ Jesus himself being the cornerstone, in whom the whole structure, being joined together, grows into a holy temple in the Lord. In him you also are being built together into a dwelling place for God by the Spirit. (Eph 2:20–22)

> As you come to him, a living stone rejected by men but in the sight of God chosen and precious, you yourselves like living stones are being built up as a spiritual house, to be a holy priesthood, to offer spiritual sacrifices acceptable to God through Jesus Christ. (1 Pt 2:4–5)

In this development then, we also name the Day of Pentecost as a descent of the glory of God, foreshadowing Jesus' return and preparing His people for it. On that day, God descended with the sound of a mighty rushing wind, and "tongues of fire appeared to them and rested on each of them and they were filled with the Holy Spirit" (Acts 2:3–4). Anointed with the Spirit of Christ, God's people are now His temple priesthood, building the reign of Jesus on earth, preparing for the day of the final return of His glory. On that day, after judgment in the glory of Jesus, all creation will once again be the temple of God.

The Glory of Christ as Fire

The Bible's predominant image for God's coming judgment in the descent of Christ's glory is fire. Fire *consumes*.

> For behold, the day is coming, burning like an oven, when all the arrogant and all evildoers will

be stubble. The day that is coming shall set them ablaze, says the Lord of hosts, so that it will leave them neither root nor branch. (Mal 4:1)

Fire purifies.

But who can endure the day of his coming, and who can stand when he appears? For he is like a refiner's fire and like fullers' soap. He will sit as a refiner and purifier of silver and will purify the sons of Levi and refine them like gold and silver. (Mal 3:2–3)

Recognizing Judgment Day as the manifestation of the glory of Jesus Christ raises these questions: How will I fare? Will all of my person and life be consumed in the fire of His glory? What will survive? How will it be tested? What of my life will be purified in that fire? How do I prepare for the coming fire of the glory of Jesus?

The Bible makes clear that there are those whose lives will be completely consumed by the fire of Christ's glory. They are those who never cherished the glory of His person, never trusted the glory of His work, never sought to obey the glory of His teachings, never aspired to the glory of His character, never set their vision upon the glorious hopes that are in Him. In no way at all was Jesus Christ their glory. They are the "weeds gathered and burned with fire" (Mt 13:40). Psalm 68 begins with a description of their plight:

God shall arise, his enemies shall be scattered; and those who hate him shall flee before him! As smoke is driven away, so you shall drive them away; as wax melts before fire, so the wicked shall perish before God! (Ps 68:1–2)

There is nothing in their lives of lasting value because it is through Jesus Christ that one enters the new creation. This is not to say that their lives are completely annihilated, for Jesus indicates "eternal punishment" awaits them (Mt 25:46), punishment that involves "weep-

ing and gnashing of teeth" (Mt 25:30). Pain, regret, and torment await
those who in no way have made Jesus Christ their glory. Their destiny
is the eternal destruction of hell (Mk 9:47–48, 2 Thes 1:9). The Bible
does not state where this suffering of hell will occur, except to say that
those sentenced to it will not be part of God's new heaven and earth.
One can only speculate that such torment will occur in dimensions of
reality outside the dimensions of the *new creation*.

In Amos 1–2, the prophet envisions the nations surrounding
Israel being thus "devoured by fire." He names Syria, Gaza, Tyre,
Edom, Ammon, Moab…and then Judah and Israel themselves being
burned up. Each of those nations had proximity to the revelation of
God's glory in the nation of Israel or, in Judah and Israel's case, had
a measure of that glory in their own Mosaic laws and national history. On account of their lack of faith, hope, and love for that glory,
they are consumed in judgment. Judgment is based on response to
the measures of the glory of Christ that each person and nation has
received. In the case of those who "go on sinning deliberately after
receiving the knowledge of the truth,"

> There no longer remains a sacrifice for sins, but a
> fearful expectation of judgment and a fury of fire
> that will consume the adversaries (of God)… For
> it is a fearful thing to fall into the hands of the
> living God. (Heb 10:26–27, 31)

The fire of Jesus Christ's glory does not consume everyone.
Others will be purified by it. For them it is a refining fire (Mal 3:3).
They are those who, to some degree, have trusted Christ's glory for
their standing with God, lived out Christ's glory in love for God and
others, and set their hopes and visions on the holiness of Jesus and
the promise of His new creation. Their promise in the fires of judgment is that they will be purified through them. The apostle Paul
describes this refinement in 1 Corinthians 3:11–15:

> No one can lay a foundation other than that
> which is laid, which is Jesus Christ. Now if any-

one builds on the foundation with gold, silver, precious stones, wood, hay, straw—each one's work will become manifest, for the Day will disclose it, because it will be revealed by fire, and the fire will test what sort of work each one has done. If the work that anyone has built on the foundation survives, he will receive a reward. If anyone's work is burned up, he will suffer loss, though he himself will be saved, but only as through fire.

Purified by fire, the entirety of one's life will be judged by the glory of Christ. He is the foundation who lasts into the new creation. This judgment includes one's deeds, thoughts, and motives of the heart.

Therefore do not pronounce judgment before the time, before the Lord comes, who will bring to light the things now hidden in darkness and will disclose the purposes of the heart. Then each one will receive his commendation from God. (1 Cor 4:5)

Thus, we will be judged not only on what we have done (Mt 25:31–46) but *why* we have done what we have done.

For God will bring every deed into judgment, with every secret thing, whether good or evil. (Eccl 12:14)

Is your life being built on the foundation of Jesus' glory in His person and work? Your thoughts? Your deeds? Your motives behind your deeds? No one can lay any foundation other than that which has been laid for the new creation, that being the glory of Jesus Christ. The grace of God in Jesus orients us toward and prepares us for the Day of Judgment.

For the grace of God has appeared, bringing salvation for all people, training us to renounce ungodliness and worldly passions, and to live self-controlled, upright, and godly lives in the present age, waiting for our blessed hope, the appearing of the glory of our great God and Savior Jesus Christ, who gave himself for us to redeem us from all lawlessness and to purify for himself a people for his own possession who are zealous for good works. (Ti 2:11–14)

Before turning to the matter of preparation for judgment, it must also be noted that not only humans will face that fire of Christ's glory—*all* of creation will pass through this refinement before entering the new creation.

The heavens and earth that now exist are stored up for fire, being kept until the day of judgment and destruction of the ungodly... But the day of the Lord will come like a thief, and then the heavens will pass away with a roar, and the heavenly bodies will be burned up and dissolved, and the earth and works that are done on it will be exposed. (2 Pt 3:7, 10)

These verses do not teach the complete destruction of the present earth but its refinement by the fire of Christ's glory (just as our earth, through the previous judgment of the flood, was not annihilated but cleansed, a fact referred to earlier in the same chapter, 2 Pt 3:6). The heavenly bodies that "dissolve" may refer to the spiritual powers that oppose God, or it may refer to the splitting of the skies in Christ's return. Either way, the earth remains even as it is purged. All its civilization and culture will be "laid bare," "made known" (alternate translations for "exposed"), and purified in the coming judgment. Thereafter, "creation itself will be set free from its bondage to decay and obtain the freedom of the glory of the children of God" (Rom 8:21).

CHAPTER 13

Preparing for Return and Judgment

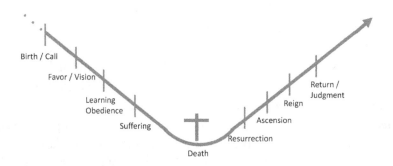

Preparing for Judgment—Cherish the Son

Because it is in the fire of Christ's glory that we are judged, preparing wisely for that Day of the Lord involves cherishing Jesus—His person, His work—building our lives upon Him in faith, hope, and love.

> For these three abide, faith, hope and love; but
> the greatest of these is love. (1 Cor 13:13)

Reading Scripture in Christ, the witness of those cherishing the Son is evidenced throughout. First Kings 3:16–28 illustrates the great divide of humanity between those who do cherish the Son and those who do not. Two prostitutes are brought before wise King Solomon, each claiming that a living son belongs to them and that a dead son doesn't. Solomon decides to split the son in half, giving each mother a portion. One mother is satisfied with this decision. The other mother who cherishes the life of the *living son* gives up her own life (i.e., her natural rights to a mother's life and its happiness) for the *son's* sake.

> Oh, my lord, give her the living child, and by no
> means put him to death. (1 Kgs 3:26)

This mother is the one who receives the life of the son beyond that Judgment Day, for she cherished his life more than her own. "Whoever does not take his cross and follow me is not worthy of me," Jesus declared. "Whoever finds his life will lose it, and whoever loses his life for my sake will find it" (Mt 10:38–39).

Back in chapter 1 of this book, when reading the Joseph story in Christ, we saw the exalted Joseph, the one who sat at Pharaoh's right hand, putting his brothers through their *judgment test*. That test, described in Genesis 42, was to determine whether they cherished the "favored son" (Benjamin by Jacob), the Son uniquely loved of the Father (Jn 5:20), the son through whom God's Abrahamic promises to their family line would continue. Would they cherish him or cavalierly dismiss him as they had done with Joseph? They do cherish him! And that cherishing leads to their union with Joseph and the inheritance of a new land of safety and abundance (Goshen).

Perhaps no one cherishes the Son more in the Old Testament than Hannah and her fellow barren women—Sara, Rachel, Naomi, and Manoah's wife. Their lives, as with the rest of mankind, only bore ultimate meaning if they were blessed with the life of a son, *the* Son. So Hannah prayed in "deep distress, weeping bitterly" (1 Sm 1:10) in the temple of the Lord. And she vowed in prayer, as all true Christians do, that if she is granted the life of a son, he will be given and dedicated to the Lord all the days of his life (v. 11). Even so, the life of *the* Son is given to believers ultimately for the glory of God. In this camp of barren women, we also recognize the Shunammite woman of 2 Kings 4:8–37. She made room for the Word of God, the prophet Elisha (v. 10). Doing so, she is miraculously gifted with the life of a son, a gift for her too great to be believed:

> No, my lord, O man of God; do not lie to your
> servant. (2 Kgs 4:16)

Can there truly be life beyond the barrenness of death, the barrenness of this age? God's Word declares it to be so! It is in the son:

> The woman conceived, and she bore a son about
> that time the following spring, as Elisha had said
> to her. (2 Kgs 4:17)

"And this is the testimony, that God gave us eternal life, and this life is in his Son. Whoever has the Son has life; whoever does not have the Son of God does not have life" (1 Jn 5:11–12). How do we know that the story of the Shunammite's son draws us to cherish the life of *the* Son, Jesus? Her son tragically dies (2 Kings 4:20), but then, hallelujah, is raised to life again by the Word of God in Elisha (v. 35)!

In the call to prepare for Judgment Day by cherishing the Son, one other Old Testament reference must be cited. It is not a verse or story or even a particular book of the Bible, though it encompasses more than one. It is the call to cherish wisdom.

> Get wisdom, get insight; do not forget her, and
> she will keep you; love her, and she will guard
> you. (Prv 4:5–6)

That call leads us to cherish Jesus Christ, His person and work, for He is the "power and wisdom of God" (1 Cor 1:24). He is the One "in whom are hidden all the treasures of wisdom and knowledge" (Col 2:3). He is the One "through whom all things were made" (Jn 1:3), so He is the wisdom embedded in creation (cf. Prv 8)—the One who existed "before the mountains had been shaped" (v. 25), the One who was "beside God, like a master workman, being daily his delight, rejoicing before him always, rejoicing in his inhabited world and delighting in the children of man." So cherishing Christ is the pursuit of wisdom that the Psalms and Proverbs and Ecclesiastes call us to. And here is the promise of that pursuit, a promise made most evident on Judgment Day:

> The beginning of wisdom is this: Get wisdom, and whatever you get, get insight. Prize her highly, and she will exalt you: she will honor you if you embrace her. She will place on your head a graceful garland; she will bestow on you a beautiful crown. (Prv 4:7–9)

Cherishing wisdom is cherishing the Son, and such pursuit will know its reward.

Faith, Hope, and Love

Faith toward the Day of Judgment begins by trusting the work of Jesus Christ for our eternal standing with God. It is understanding and cherishing the glory of His obedience for our righteousness before God and our justification with Him, an obedience even unto death on a cross (Phil 2:8). In Jesus then, "a righteousness of God has been manifested apart from the law, although the Law and the Prophets bear witness to it" (Rom 3:21). Faith renounces self-righteousness before God because "all have sinned and fall short of His glory" (v. 23). Faith confesses in the sorrow of repentance a need for Jesus' righteousness and gives thanks that "through our Lord Jesus Christ we have now received reconciliation" (Rom 5:11). This knowledge and trust, cherishing Jesus, is entrance into God's kingdom.

Faith further grows an identity in Christ Jesus from which lives are transformed. Cherishing Jesus as one's Savior from the just punishment of God's wrath leads a Christian to then continue to cherish Him in faith as Lord. This is the journey of sanctification. The apostle Paul calls us to turn from sin in the power of our new identity.

> Do not present your members to sin as instruments of unrighteousness, but present your-

selves to God as those who have been brought from death to life, and your members to God as instruments for righteousness. For sin will have no dominion over you, since you are not under law but under grace. (Rom 6:13–14)

This journey prepares us for the Day of Judgment, the righteousness of Jesus being not only our ground of justification but the substance of our sanctification. Paul himself describes his journey out of covetousness (Rom 7:7) into Christ. Covetousness of anything, even religious admiration, must diminish if Jesus is to grow in us. Thus, in Philippians 3:2–11, Paul considers his religious pedigree and effort as "loss" (v. 7) and "rubbish" (v. 8) for the sake of Christ. It is loss because to whatever degree it exists as a pride in his identity, it diminishes in him the "surpassing worth of knowing Christ Jesus his Lord" (v. 8). Therefore, with his sights set clearly on Judgment Day, Paul lives to be found thoroughly in Christ:

> Not having a righteousness of my own that comes from the law, but that which comes through faith in Christ, the righteousness from God that depends on faith—that I may know him and the power of his resurrection and may share his sufferings, becoming like him in his death, that by any means possible I may attain the resurrection from the dead. Not that I have already obtained this or am already perfect, but I press on to make it my own, because Christ Jesus has made me his own. Brothers, I do not consider that I have made it my own. But one thing I do: forgetting what lies behind and straining forward to what lies ahead, I press on toward the goal for the prize of the upward call of God in Christ Jesus. Let those of us who are mature think this way. (Phil 3:9–15)

This is how faith cherishes Jesus in preparation for the purifying fires of His glory on the Day of Judgment.

Hope cherishes Jesus in vision, both personal and social—vision that we live toward as we prepare for judgment. Hope cherishes the beauty of Jesus' person.

> One thing I have asked of the Lord, that will I seek after: that I may dwell in the house of the Lord all the days of my life, to gaze upon the beauty of the Lord and to inquire in his temple. (Ps 27:4)

Blogger David Sliker gives an example of how hope cherishes the person of Jesus:

> One of the most fascinating things to ponder about Jesus is what it would be like to know a Man who had no trace of cynicism, pessimism, world-weary, worn-down complaint and unfulfilled bitterness related to regret or offense or petty spite. He is a Man with no insecurity, no need for our approval, or any desire to use us for His own emotional gain or personal benefit. He loves and enjoys us with a free heart with no brokenness… What would it be like to experience the full spectrum of the pain and the messiness of the human condition, yet remain fresh and vibrant, bursting with the hope of new possibilities connected to an endless fountain of delight and wonder? (DavidSliker.com, Facebook post, May 17, 2020)

This is hope in action, cherishing the person of Jesus, and such hope transforms our lives, prepares us for *judgment*, and is prelude to the rewards of heavenly life. Sliker continues,

> What's astonishing to me is that the interior life of the Holy Spirit offers us the invitation to both

know Jesus in this way now and repent and reach for the grace to experience this ourselves. We can have the cynicism, the weariness, the bitterness washed from our hearts today. We can experience the freshness of a life unspoiled and the renewal of joy unspeakable, if we want. That is the beauty and glory of what the life of Christ offers to us—daily and continually—as we drink of His streams of living waters.

Cherishing Jesus in this way will know its fullest reward in life beyond Judgment Day. In the age to come, all of our thirsts in Christ find their ultimate quenching. On that day,

> the Spirit and the Bride say, "Come." And let the one who hears say, "Come." And let the one who is thirsty come; let the one who desires take the water of life without price. (Rv 22:17)

When we cherish Jesus in hope, our longings in Him are not only personal. They, too, are social, political, cultural, and global. Cherishing Jesus, we hope toward God's shalom kingdom of justice and beauty, human safety, provision, and flourishing on earth. After Zacchaeus met Jesus and was called into the kingdom of heaven, he pursued justice and generosity:

> Behold, Lord, the half of my goods I give to the poor. And if I have defrauded anyone of anything, I restore it fourfold. (Luke 19:8)

Having met Jesus, Zacchaeus' sights were set on that city "that has foundations, whose designer and builder is God" (Heb 11:10). The church corporately finds its eternal identity in being a sign of that city, a sign of the kingdom. Cherishing Jesus, we become "ambassadors for Christ with a message of reconciliation in this world" (2 Cor 5:20). This is done not only in the cause of reconciliation between mankind and God but also mankind with each other. Christ is the power of unity and peace (Eph 2:14). The ministry of reconciliation is done toward the day of full reconciliation to come, when heaven and earth are made fully one again. Therefore, Christians cherish Jesus in hopes that are social, cultural, and global and, like those personal, these hopes, too, will know their reward on the day of His coming in glory. In that day of the new heavens and earth,

> the glory and honor of the nations will be brought
> into the city (Rv 21:26),

the New Jerusalem.

To the four cardinal virtues of *classical* antiquity—prudence, justice, fortitude, and temperance—the church, to parallel its number of deadly sins (seven), added the three theological and biblical virtues of faith, hope, and love, and "the greatest of these is love." Love cherishes Jesus Christ in deed and motive. Love in deed authenticates true faith in Jesus (Jas 2:17). Love in deed evidences a cherishing of the Jesus who became incarnate for our salvation. Hence, in Jesus' description of Judgment Day (Mt 25:31–46), those who fed the hungry, gave drink to the thirsty, welcomed the stranger, clothed the naked, visited the sick and imprisoned are brought into His eternal kingdom. Not that those deeds in themselves save us but our love of Jesus within those deeds does.

> For in as much as you have done it to one of the
> least of these my brothers, you did it to me. (Mt
> 25:40)

For this reason, both deed and motive matter. Self-congratulatory, self-affirming, self-glorifying motives in even the best of works are purged in the fire of Jesus' glory. To prepare for judgment, Christians learn to love in faith with thanksgiving, freedom, and joy. Christians learn to love toward our hopes, both personal and social, in order to cherish Christ in deed and motive. Only this love abides an will know its reward in the age to come.

Versus Decisionism

It should be evident by now that preparation for Judgment Day is not simply a matter of *making a decision for Jesus*. Yes, a decision to honor and trust Jesus' glory begins life in His kingdom, but thereafter, Judgment Day is prepared for through numerous decisions for Jesus. It is prepared for by asking, Who am I becoming in preparation to meet Jesus' glory? Who am I becoming in the freedom and grace of Jesus? How much of the glory of Christ is growing in me? How many of my values and trusts will survive the fire of His glory? What parts of my identity yet exist at the expense of knowing myself in Christ? How deep are my longings in Christ—for myself as a person, for my world and its needs? Who am I living toward, a vision of myself in Christ or a vision of myself according to worldly comfort? What am I living toward, a vision of God's kingdom or a vision of worldly values?

1 Corinthians 3:14–15 affirms,

> If the work that anyone has built on the foundation (of Christ's glory) survives, he will receive a reward. If anyone's work is burned up, he will suffer loss, though he himself will be saved, but only as through fire.

Clearly, there will be "bigger" and "smaller" people in the age to come, even as one's faith, hope, and love finds its reward in and through the Judgment Day. Some have lived deeply and fully for the Day and Age of the Revelation of Jesus' glory, others minimally. Jesus himself affirms this in His parable of the ten minas in Luke 19:11–27. Each of the nobleman's servants received ten minas (a mina = three months' wages) prior to their Lord's departure. Upon his return, they are called to account for what they have done with these measures of His glory. One servant doubled his minas; a second increased them by 50 percent; a third kept his laid away in a hand-kerchief. Each servant is then rewarded with how they cultivated the measure of glory given to them. Their reward beyond the judgment encounter is described as "having authority over ten cities and five cities," respectively. Their increase in faith, hope, and love in this age leads to increase in authority in the next, authority constituting leadership, responsibility, ability, gifting, and influence. The third servant is condemned as wicked, and his minas are taken away. Such are the natural rewards of Judgment Day and the life to come. Some will be richer and greater in the glory of Christ, others less so, and some empty. Who are you becoming in preparation for His return in glory?

If mankind is each judged and cleansed by Christ's glory, one may wonder, *Will that then lead us each to be alike?* Not at all. In fact, it is just the opposite. We will know our unique and true selves after the cleansing of Christ's glory. C. S. Lewis explains this using the illustration of light as representative of Jesus' glory. He writes,

> Imagine a lot of people who have always lived in the dark. You come and try to describe to them what light is like. You might tell them that if they come into the light that same light would fall on them all and they would all reflect it and thus become what we call visible. Is it not quite possible that they would imagine that, since they were all receiving the same light, and all reacting to it in the same way (i.e., all reflecting it), they would all look alight? Whereas you and I know that the light will in fact bring out or show up, how different they are… In that sense our real selves are all waiting for us in Him. (*Mere Christianity*, pp 224–225)

So let's pursue the knowledge of our true selves toward that Day of Light.

What of Those Who Have Never Heard?

It is incumbent on the followers of Jesus to share the glory of His person and work with every tribe and nation, for He Himself is the foundation of God's new creation. Jesus said,

> All authority in heaven and on earth has been given to me. Go therefore and make disciples of all nations, baptizing them in the name of the Father and of the Son and of the Holy Spirit, teaching them to observe all that I have commanded you. And behold, I am with you always, to the end of the age. (Mt 28:18–20)

But what of those who have never heard of Jesus? It is important to recognize that Jesus' glory is not something absolutely foreign to any person. Every person encounters a measure of the glory of Christ in both creation and natural law, including the norms of creation. This is the apostle Paul's teaching in Romans 1–2. Because creation was made through the Son, His "eternal power and divine nature are clearly perceived in the things that have been made" (1:20). This renders all mankind responsible and "without excuse" (1:20) on the Day of Judgment. In creation, the glory of Christ is evident in its majesty, beauty, order, provision, and power. In creation, the glory of Christ is also evident in its norms of gender, marriage, family, even social-cultural realities like education, politics, art, and business. All of this glory renders every person liable in response.

Christ's glory, too, is evident in the "laws written on the hearts of all mankind" (Rom 2:15) so that "their conscience bears witness, and their conflicting thoughts will accuse or even excuse them on the day when, according to the gospel, God judges the secrets of men by Christ Jesus" (Rom 2:16). Our conscience and the innate laws of right and wrong bear witness to Jesus because He is the Righteousness of God. He is the human embodiment and fulfillment of God's laws (Mt 5:17). Hence, even the innate human principles of right and wrong bear witness to the glory of Jesus, and each person is accountable in their response to it.

Therefore, for those who've never heard of Jesus, nor received any of the special revelation of Scripture, their situation on the day when He comes in fullness of glory is actually no different than those who have heard of Him. Each will be judged by how they have responded to those measures of His glory that they have received in this age. (Thus, Jesus' parable of the talents [Mt 25:14–30] where some have received five talents, some two, some one measure of His glory.) What matters more than how much one has received of His glory is what you have done with the measure that you have received.

Jesus' beauty, truth, and goodness are evident in creation and natural law. For those who have responded to that glory in love, seeking to return that love to their Maker and fellowman, they, too, shall have their reward. For those who have responded to their conscience by recognizing in sorrow that they fall morally short of the glory revealed in one's innate sense of right and wrong, their reward in meeting Jesus' glory on the Day of Judgment will be to learn that His glory includes the mercy of forgiveness. For those who have cherished and lived out the glory of Christ in creation and conscience for the sake of truth, beauty, and goodness itself and not for self-serving reasons, then on the Day of Judgment they will learn that there is a Person from whom that Glory is derived, a Person they will gravitate to in love and thanks, entering His kingdom. The Apostle Paul states these truths in Romans 2:6–11:

> God will render to each one according to his works: to those who by patience in well-doing seek for glory and honor and immortality, he will give eternal life; but for those who are self-seeking and do not obey the truth, but obey unrighteousness, there will be wrath and fury. There will be trouble and distress for every human being who does evil, the Jew first and also the Greek, but glory and honor and peace for everyone who

does good, the Jew first and also the Greek. For
God shows no partiality.

This explanation of accountability for those who have never
heard of Jesus' glory should not in any way lessen the zeal to share
that glory by those who, through the witness of Holy Scripture, have
been entrusted with its knowledge. We should and must because
the more clearly and fully His glory can be shared and received, the
better all the world can respond in preparation for the Day of His
Return and even hasten that day to come (1 Pt 3:12). In the words
of Psalm 24, Christians want to call to all the world unto that day:

Lift up your heads, O gates! And lift them up, O
ancient doors, that the King of glory may come
in. Who is this King of glory? The Lord of hosts,
He is the King of glory. (Ps 24:9–10)

CHAPTER 14

Reunion and the New Creation

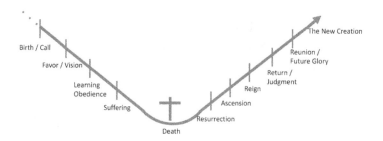

Jesus' return in glory and His final judgment are not the end of creation's story. That event is penultimate to the new creation wherein the glory of God in Christ is its "all in all" (1 Cor 15:28). The reunion of heaven (God space) and earth (human space) is the big-picture story of the Bible. It has already begun in Jesus. That is the impact of His life, death, resurrection, and ascension. "Behold, the Kingdom of God is at hand," Jesus announced at the outset of his public ministry (Mk 1:15). So as it is said, "Jesus did not come to bring us to heaven; He came to bring heaven on earth." This good news is entered through repentance and faith. "Repent and believe in the gospel" (Mk 1:15). In Christ Jesus, therefore, the new creation has begun, and we are preparing for the day of its fullness in glory when heaven and earth are fully united.

And He who was seated on the throne said,
"Behold, I am making all things new." (Rv 21:5)

In Jesus, therefore, Christians are already, through faith, a "new
creation" (2 Cor 5:17), living toward the fullness of their glory as
humans in the new creation of our universe. The kingdom is both
now and not yet. The *not yet* is the fullness of "glory union" between
heaven and earth that we live toward.

The Beauty of Union

> See what kind of love the Father has given to us,
> that we should be called children of God; and so
> we are. The reason why the world does not know
> us is that it did not know him. Beloved, we are
> God's children now and what we will be has not
> yet appeared; but we know that when he appears
> we shall be like him, because we shall see him as
> he is. And everyone who thus hopes in him puri-
> fies himself as he is pure. (1 Jn 3:1–3)

Full personal union with the glory of Jesus is set before
Christians as our great hope and vision. It is the power to pursue
purity, for if the glory of righteousness is the destiny of our life and
our truest identity, let us live toward it now! Impurity is a distraction,
a diversion, and a denial of a Christian's destiny. To anticipate this
Day of Full Union does not negate the fact that our union with Jesus
has already begun. Already, in this age, we are "sealed with his Holy
Spirit" (Eph 1:13–14), who is

> the guarantee of our inheritance until we acquire
> possession of it, to the praise of his glory.

Our beginnings in union with Christ are preparing us for our
full inheritance!

Reading Scripture in Christ, the paradigm used for this Day of Union is marriage, Jesus' return likened to a wedding day.

> "Hallelujah! For the Lord our God the Almighty reigns. Let us rejoice and exult and give him the glory, for the marriage of the Lamb has come, and his Bride has made herself ready; it was granted her to clothe herself with fine linen, bright and pure"—for the fine linen is the righteous deeds of the saints. And the angel said to me, "Write this: Blessed are those who are invited to the marriage supper of the Lamb." And he said to me, "These are the true words of God." (Rv 19:6–9)

In this marriage paradigm, the sacrament of baptism, administered within the covenant relationship between God and His people, is best understood as a marriage proposal. "Will you be mine?" God in Jesus asks His people individually and personally in baptism. (And He did not just go down on His knee to make this proposal; He went all the way down to death on a cross, down to the anguish of hell to meet you there to ask!) Administered to a child, the people of God then, led by that child's parents, introduce the child to her Suitor, encouraging her to say yes to His proposal. Profession of faith and its commitment then "engage" that person to Jesus. It is saying yes to God's covenant proposal in Jesus. Thereafter, a life of faithfulness and honor to our "Fiancé" is pursued in this age, all anticipating the wedding and marriage and Day of Full Union to come!

Psalm 45 speaks to that Day. Addressing the Groom King:

> You are the most handsome of the sons of men; grace is poured upon your lips; therefore God has blessed you forever. Gird your sword on your thigh, O mighty one, in your splendor and majesty. (Ps 45:2–3)

And addressing the *bride*:

> Hear, O daughter, and consider, and incline your
> ear: forget your people and your father's house,
> and the king will desire your beauty. Since he is
> your lord, bow to him... All glorious is the prin-
> cess in her chamber, with robes interwoven with
> gold... With joy and gladness they are led along
> as they enter the palace of the king. (Ps 45:10–15)

What a day of glory and beauty to live toward!

Theologically, the apostle Paul also describes our union with Christ with the language of marriage. Citing Genesis 2:24, Paul teaches that human marriage, in fact, finds its meaning and calling in the union of Jesus with His people.

> Therefore a man shall leave his father and mother
> and hold fast to his wife, and the two shall
> become one flesh. This mystery is profound,
> and I am saying that it refers to Christ and the
> church. (Eph 5:31–32)

Paul understands the incarnation in the light of marriage, Christ and His body united as one flesh. He also teaches a husband's and wife's calling in marriage within this union paradigm.

> Husbands, love your wives, as Christ loved the
> church and gave himself up for her, that he might
> sanctify her... Wives, submit to your own hus-
> bands, as to the Lord. For the husband is the
> head of the wife even as Christ is the head of the
> church, his body. (Eph 5:25–26, 22–23)

This view of marriage leads to the understanding of Genesis 2:18–25 as a foreshadowing of the Day of Full Union to come— between Jesus, the second Adam, and His bride, the church. "It is not good for man to be alone; I will make a helper fit for him," the Lord God declares (v. 18). So the Lord God caused a deep sleep to fall upon the man and, while he slept, took one of his ribs and closed up its place with flesh. The "deep sleep" of Jesus took Him to the cross where His side was pierced (Jn 19:34)—blood and water flowing from that side to form His bride. Then the first Adam is "awakened" (resurrection/ascension) from his sleep so that he could receive the bride that the Lord God brings to him (v. 22).

> This at last is bone of my bones and flesh of my flesh; she shall be called Woman, because she was taken out of Man. (Gn 2:22)

Christians affirm the "resurrection of the body" (cf. Luke 24:39) toward the Day of Union because our Groom Himself became incarnate for that day. Then the Genesis 2 passage ends with this description of the beauty of full union's intimacy:

> And the man and his wife were both naked and were not ashamed. (Gn. 2:25)

In that Day of Union, all of Jesus' people are cleansed from shame. The guilt of sin has been atoned for by His pierced side, but the power of sin remains with us in our mortal bodies throughout this age with its temptations and shames. Hallelujah, there will be a day of complete freedom from those shameful powers of sin, a day we will inherit our resurrected body, a day of personal glory and true beauty in union with the Savior.

Because of the paradigm of marriage, this joy of union is also witnessed to in the Song of Solomon. That Bible book celebrates the blessings of marital union, even its physical joys.

> My beloved is mine and I am his. (Sg 2:16)

To be sure, the bliss of human marital union is the subject of this book, but through it, like the other Scripture passages about marriage, the union between Christ and His church is witnessed to. The Song deepens us in longing for that Day of Full Union:

> On my bed by night I sought him whom my soul loves; I sought him, but found him not. I will rise now and go about the city, in the streets and in the squares; I will seek him whom my soul loves. The watchmen found me as they went about in the city. "Have you seen him whom my soul loves?" Scarcely had I passed them when I found him whom my soul loves. I held him, and would not let him go. (Sg 3:1–4)

The Rewards of Union

If the heart of the new creation is union with the glory of Christ Jesus, it is not difficult to understand the promised rewards of the age to come. They are natural rewards in accordance with the measures of faith, hope, and love that we have cultivated in this age toward that day. They are in accord with *sowing* and *reaping*:

> The one who sows to the Spirit will from the Spirit reap eternal life. Let us not grow weary of doing good, for in due season we will reap, if we do not give up. (Gal 6:9–10)

In other words, the more we sow to life in the Spirit through trusting Christ, longing for His glory, living out His love, the more we will reap as joy and strength and depth of life in Christ when He is all in all.

> Love your enemies, and do good, and lend, expecting nothing in return, and your reward will be great, and you will be sons of the Most High, for he is kind to the ungrateful and the

evil. Be merciful, even as your father is merciful.
(Luke 6:35)

Growing into the character of Christ today will find its satisfaction and fullness of meaning in the new creation. Like a pen pal of
days gone by, writing, learning of, imitating, growing close to another
person via letters will know its natural reward when comes the day of
meeting face-to-face. The same glass of water brings deeper joy and
satisfaction to those who are thirstier. Faith, hope, and love cultivate
a thirst for Jesus to be rewarded with varying depths of satisfaction
on the Day of Union:

> Let the one who is thirsty come; let the one who
> desires take the water of life without price. (Rv
> 22:17)

But the rewards of that Day will not just be in personal satisfaction. They will also be in the fellowship of Christ's will, in depth
of love to carry it forth. Hence, in Jesus' parables preparing His people for the Day of His return (Luke 19:11–27, Mt 25:14–30), Jesus
rewards those who have worked well with their investments of His
glory with "authority" (Luke 19:17) and influence:

> You have been faithful over a little; I will set you
> over much. Enter into the joy of your master.
> (Mt 25:23)

Through faith, hope, and love in Christ Jesus, we gain currency
and leadership for the age of union to come.

Therefore, the Scriptures call us to *eagerly* wait for the day of Jesus'
return (the idea of reward being contained within our "eagerness").

> Christ, having been offered once to bear the sins
> of many, will appear a second time, not to deal
> with sin but to save those who are eagerly waiting
> for him. (Heb 9:28)

Likewise, when we face the trials of this age, we view them through the lens of eternal reward.

> We do not lose heart. Though our outer nature is wasting away, our inner nature is being renewed day by day. For this slight momentary affliction is preparing for us an eternal weight of glory beyond comparison, as we look not to the things that are seen but to the things that are unseen. For the things that are seen are transient, but the things that are unseen are eternal. (2 Cor 4:16–18)

Faith, hope, and love are deepened in the challenges of this life in this age, preparing us for the rewards of Christ's glory.

The same applies to the promised resurrection of the body. It is "sown in dishonor, but will be raised in glory" (1 Cor 15:43). Philippians 3:20 adds,

> Our citizenship is in heaven, and from it we await a Savior, the Lord Jesus Christ, who will transform our lowly body to be like his glorious body, by the power that enables him even to subject all things to himself.

Will the rewards of heaven translate to our future resurrected bodies? Will the promise of heavenly reward in Christ be translated physically (i.e., those with more maturity/authority/influence and those with less)? If that is so, we might then anticipate seeing babies, children, teens, and adults in resurrection glory, along with the hope of continued heavenly growth (expressed physically) in that glory. One can only speculate how the natural rewards of heaven will manifest themselves physically, but we can be confident that our physical selves will manifest our true and unique identities in Christ Jesus cultivated in this current age.

The New Earth

> Blessed are the meek, for they shall inherit the earth. (Mt 5:5)

In His beatitude, Jesus promises those who learn to be loved and led by God in Himself, those who cultivate the strength of meekness, they will inherit the earth! The new creation that Jesus brings to His people is a "new heaven [God space] and new earth [man space]" (Rv 21:1). It is the fulfillment of Isaiah's vision,

> For behold, I create new heavens and a new earth, and the former things shall not be remembered or come into mind... No more shall there be in it an infant who lives but a few days, or an old man who does not fill out his days... They shall build houses and inhabit them; they shall plant vineyards and eat their fruit... The wolf and the lamb shall graze together; the lion shall eat straw like the ox, and dust shall be the serpent's food. They shall not hurt or destroy in all my holy mountain," says the Lord. (Is 65:17, 20–21, 25)

The prophet Amos, too, foresaw this future for God's people:

> "Behold, the days are coming," declares the Lord, "when the plowman shall overtake the reaper and the treader of grapes him who sows the seed; the mountains shall drip sweet wine, and all the hills shall flow with it. I will restore the fortunes of my people Israel, and they shall rebuild the ruined cities and inhabit them; they shall plant vineyards and drink their wine, and they shall make gardens and eat their fruit. I will plant them on their land, and they shall never again be uprooted out of the land that I have given them," says the Lord. (Am 9:13–15)

190

"I will plant them on their land"—how this needs to be said to the people of God in our day. So many Christians have grown up with a Gnostic/Platonic/otherworldly vision of our future, gained through the hymns we've sung, a vision contrary to a new earth! "Some glad morning when this life is o'er / I'll fly away / To a home on God's celestial shore / I'll fly away." God's people don't fly away; we get to stay! We inherit the earth. "To the old rugged Cross / I will ever be true / its shame and reproach gladly bear / Then He'll call me someday to my home far away / where His glory forever I'll share." Our home is not "far away"; it's the earth that we're standing on. True, not the earth in its current nature; our earth must be yet purified and filled with Christ's glory. But the land, earth is our home! It shall not "dissolve like snow" (contemporary version of "Amazing Grace"). Christians are the ones who get to stay on the good earth.

Another manifestation of this misteaching can be seen in obituary notices. It is common to read of a Christian who dies that they have gone to their "heavenly home." That is not a biblical vision of life beyond the grave. More accurately, the believer who passes out of this age goes to their "heavenly rest," awaiting the Resurrection Day when they will enter their heavenly home—the new heaven and earth! These false ideas have led popular culture to envision life beyond this age as ethereal, cloudlike (hence, more Gnostic or Platonic, i.e., the soul escaping from the evil body and material world). They, too, have propagated the idea that those who have died regularly communicate and fellowship as spirits with those of us yet in this age of the earth. There may be some of that as God would specially ordain (i.e., Moses and Elijah with Jesus on the Mount of Transfiguration), but the dominant image of the believer's intermediate state is *sleep/rest*.

> Blessed are the dead who die in the Lord, that
> they may rest from their labors, for their deeds
> follow them. (Rv 14:13)

A believer's deeds "follow them," awaiting the return of Jesus to earth, the resurrection of the body and Judgment Day...and the new earth—into which their deeds find meaning and fulfillment.

Because earth is the inheritance of Jesus' people, God's salvation promises to Abram take on meaning to those in new covenant relationship with God, a meaning similar to Abram's. In Genesis 12:1, God calls Abram to journey toward a promised land:

> Now the Lord said to Abram, "Go from your country and your kindred and your father's house to the LAND I will show you."

Reading Scripture in Christ, this is the journey that all Christians are on. Genesis 15:18–21 further defines this promised land of the Old Covenant:

> On that day the Lord made a covenant with Abram, saying, "To your offspring I give this land from the river of Egypt to the great river, the river Euphrates, the land of the Kenites, the Kenizzites, the Kadmonites, the Hittities, the Perizzites, the Rephaim, the Amorites, the Canaanites, the Girgashites and the Jebusites. (Gn 15:18–21)

In coming to fulfill the Old Covenant, Jesus does not remove the promise of land. He expands it to now include the whole earth and, perhaps, in the farther future, even the entire universe!

Reading Scripture in Christ, we also recognize that the earth we inherit is now yet populated with ungodliness—as the promised land was for Abram's offspring. But led by our Joshua (Jesus), we take on those forces of ungodliness as we begin to enter our promised inheritance. God's promise to Joshua on the verge of Canaan, therefore, is a promise He makes to Jesus, a promise in which those in Christ find hope for life in this age:

> Moses my servant is dead [the Old Covenant]. Now therefore arise, go over this Jordan [death], you and all this people [believers], into the land I am giving to them, to the people of Israel. Every

place that the sole of your foot will tread upon I
have given to you, just as I promised to Moses…
No man shall be able to stand before you all the
days of your life. Just as I was with Moses, so
I will be with you. I will not leave you or forsake you. Be strong and courageous, for you shall
cause this people to inherit the land that I swore
to their fathers to give them. (Jo. 1:2–6)

In this Word, Christians go forward to battle ungodliness,
claiming the earth as our inheritance, obeying God, following our
captain, Jesus, seeking to claim the earth for God because we know
our promised land is a "good and broad land, a land flowing with
milk and honey" (Ex 3:8).

When ungodliness has been purged from the earth, and its government is fully under the lordship of Jesus Christ, then will come
the fulfillment of the prophetic visions of Habakkuk and Ezekiel.

For the EARTH will be filled with the knowledge
of the glory of the Lord as the waters cover the
sea. (Hb 2:14)

My servant David shall be king over them, and
they shall all have one shepherd. They shall walk
in my rules and be careful to obey my statutes.
They shall dwell in the LAND that I gave to my
servant Jacob, where your fathers lived. They and
their children and their children's children shall
dwell there forever, and David my servant will
be their prince forever. I will make a covenant of
peace with them. It shall be an everlasting covenant with them. And I will set them in their LAND
and multiply them, and will set my sanctuary in
their midst forevermore. My dwelling place shall
be with them, and I will be their God, and they
shall be my people. Then the nations will know

that I am the Lord who sanctifies Israel, when
my sanctuary is in their midst. (Ez 37:24–28, cf.
also Rv 21:3)

Some Implications

Because the new earth is our promised land, Christians cherish
the good earth—the smell of its soil, the colors of fall, the call of the
loon, the tastes of the vine. It is noteworthy that Abram, after being
given the call "to go to a place he was to receive as an inheritance"
(Heb 11:8), "went out to that place."

> By faith he went to live in the land of promise,
> as in a foreign land, living in tents with Isaac and
> Jacob, heirs with him of the same promise. For
> he was looking forward to the city that has foun-
> dations whose designer and builder is God. (Heb
> 11:9–10)

Just as Abram moved into the promised land, so Christians
"move into" this earth. It is our inheritance, and though we don't
receive it until the next age of the earth, we nevertheless live on it
as if it is ours! We plant our lives like a seed into this earth, even
as our Lord Jesus did (Jn 12:24). This not only refers to cherishing
its nature but also developing culture and investing in civilization
toward its glorious future (see later section, "The New City").

Christians, too, care for the earth and the world it contains. We
care for its environment as an expression of the Word of God and
glory of Christ. God spoke the earth into being (Gn 1). It is made
through the Son who is God's Eternal Word, the Word who became
incarnate for our salvation. In this salvation, Jesus also used the paradigm of pregnancy and birth to explain how the world today holds
its future, the kingdom of God, in its womb, like a mother with child
(Mt 24:8, cf. Chapter 11 of this book entitled, "Reign: Opposition
and Triumph"). This analogy carries in it another vision for caring
for our world, for the best way to care for a child in the womb is

to care for its mother through good nutrition and exercise, giving emotional, educational, and spiritual nourishment as well. Thus, Christians care for the world, and in a similar vein, Christians honor and care for their bodies (1 Cor 6:12–20) knowing that there will be a resurrection of the body.

The promise of the new heavens and earth also implies that there will be another "age" of our earth. This recognition makes Christians much more comfortable with the scientific geological evidence that our earth has had numerous ages in its 4.6-billion-year history. There are technical terms for this; broadly speaking, earth's eras are divided into the Paleozoic, Mesozoic, and Cenozoic. The Mesozoic, or "Middle Life" era, is the one which featured giant reptiles, dinosaurs, and other monstrous beasts. It is sometimes called the Age of Dinosaurs. It ended, most scientists agree, with a dramatic "coming"—the coming of an asteroid. The asteroid's impact created so much dust that the sun was blocked, halting photosynthesis. Consequently, the dinosaurs lost their food source and became extinct. This then led to next age of the earth. In a similar way, Christians contend that there will be another "coming" to end our current age of the earth—the coming of the Son of Man in glory. And like the dinosaurs, not all will survive that Coming into the next age of the earth. The dinosaur story is a warning to all people to prepare for Christ's return lest, like them, one's fate becomes extinction from the next age of the good earth.

The New Humanity

To prepare a humanity for the next age of the earth is the reason the eternal Son of God became incarnate in Jesus the Christ. Jesus is the new humanity. He is the "Everlasting Man" (G. K. Chesterton). Jesus is the true human whose life abides into the next age of our earth. He is the "firstfruit" of the new creation (1 Cor 15:20). His life is greater than death. Jesus is the "Eternal Man," as He prayed in John 17:3, "And this is eternal life, that they know you the only true God, and Jesus Christ whom you have sent."

As Jesus implies in that prayer, He is not only the Eternal Life, He has come to usher others into that Life true to our earth's next age. Those so ushered are they who "know" Him as Savior and Lord. In Jesus, humanity can become a new creation even in this current age of the earth!

> Therefore, if anyone is in Christ, he is a new creation. The old has passed away; behold, the new has come. (2 Cor 5:17)

> Of his own will he brought us forth by the word of truth, that we should be a kind of firstfruits of his creatures. (Jas 1:18)

In Jesus, Christians, too, are "firstfruits" of the new creation, already today! We are a new breed of humanity—the forever people! It is as C. S. Lewis states in his book *Mere Christianity*:

> I have called Christ the "first instance" of the new man. But of course He is something much more than that. He is not merely a new man, one specimen of the species, but *the* new man. He is the origin and center and life of all the new men. He came into the created universe, of His own will, bringing with Him the *Zoe*, the new life. (I mean new to us, of course: in its own place *Zoe* has existed for ever and ever.) And He transmits it not by heredity but by what I have called "good infection." Everyone who gets it gets it by personal contact with Him. Other men become "new" by being "in Him." (*Mere Christianity*, p. 221)

Lewis describes the process of becoming the new breed of humanity as the result of "good infection" from Jesus Christ. That infection comes through repentance and faith. Repentance is the act of dying to self. It is dying to self-righteousness, trusting alone the beauty of Jesus' life for one's standing with God. It is dying to self-will, seeking day by day to live true to Jesus, the eternal life. To become part of the humanity being bred for the new earth, one can and must choose death today and each day for Jesus' sake.

> "If anyone would come after me, let him deny himself and take up his cross and follow me," Jesus said, "For whoever would save his life will lose it, but whoever loses his life for my sake will find it." (Mt 16:24–25)

And this life of repentance continues throughout this age as Christians "evolve" (you might put it) toward the new earth, becoming "fit" for it (yes, life is a story of survival of the fittest, those "fit in Christ"). As the apostle Paul writes, "I have been crucified with Christ. It is no longer I who live, but Christ who lives in me. And the life I now live in the flesh I live by faith in the Son of God, who loved me and gave himself for me." Paul also describes this life of evolving sanctification as "putting off" the lingering ways of the "old self" in the light of one's new identity in Jesus. The "old self" is crucified—it is dead in terms of a Christian's identity. However, its thoughts, habits, and ways linger with us in our mortal bodies throughout our time in this age of the earth.

> We know that our old self was crucified with him in order that the body of sin might be brought to nothing, so that we would no longer be enslaved to sin. (Rom 6:6)

> Do not lie to one another, seeing that you have put off the old self with its practices and have put on the new self, which is being renewed in knowledge after the image of its creator. (Col 3:9–10)

Infected by Jesus, Christians are evolving into the new humanity fit for the new earth. May your evolution reach far in preparation for the future!

The calling of Jesus to create a new humanity fit for the new earth also sheds light on the biblical accounts of human origins. For reflections on this, see Appendix 1.

The New City

Biblically, the new creation ends in a new city.

> Then I saw a new heaven and a new earth, for the first heaven and the first earth had passed away, and the sea was no more. And I saw the holy city, new Jerusalem coming down out of heaven from God, prepared as a bride adorned for her husband. (Rv 21:1–2)

It is vital for Christians to fix this vision in their spiritual sites because a city implies a civilization with culture and society. This city vision is what those in Christ live toward—like their Father Abraham.

> By faith Abraham obeyed when he was called to go out to a place that he was to receive as an inheritance... For he was looking forward to the city that has foundations, whose designer and builder is God. (Heb 11:8, 10)

The New Jerusalem is the consummation of human civilization. Cultures build upon each other, using insights and technologies from earlier cultures. The New Jerusalem does not replace the developments of previous human civilizations; it fulfills them. In the words of Acts 3:21, it "restores" them.

> Repent therefore, and turn back, that your sins may be blotted out, that times of refreshing may

come from the presence of the Lord, and that he may send the Christ appointed for you, Jesus, whom heaven must receive until the time for restoring all the things about which God spoke by the mouth of his holy prophets long ago. (Acts 3:19–21)

The overarching narrative of the Bible is the development of our earth from a *garden* to a *city*. Created and breathed into, mankind, as the image of God on earth, was called to "have dominion" (Gn 1:28) over the earth, ruling in holy fellowship with God. This creation mandate came prior to mankind's fall into sin. It involved four tasks: to *fill* and *rule*,

Be fruitful and multiply and fill the earth and subdue it and have dominion over the fish of the seas and over the birds of the heavens and over every living thing that moves on the earth (Gn 1:28),

and to *work* (till) and *keep* (guard) the special garden into which mankind was placed,

The Lord God took the man and put him in the garden of Eden to work it and keep it. (Gn 2:15)

As David Hegeman states in his book *Plowing in Hope*,

In these four tasks—ruling, filling, working, and keeping—we see culture in seed form. Human beings were called to transform the original garden into a beautiful city, which is the eventual goal of human history as revealed in the final pages of the Bible. This comprehensive transformation was possible only when human beings formed communities where a wide diversity of

talents and skills could be developed and pooled
together in order to complete the monumental
cultural task—to the glory of God. (p. 26)

This cultivation of the good, yet "empty", earth into a God-
glorifying city need not come at the expense of the natural world's
splendor. It is integrated into it. Hegeman again:

Ideally, mankind's culturative transformation of
the earth should work in harmony with God's
original creation order. The goal is to create a
"Garden-City," where the beauty of man-made
works and the glory of nature are wed in a mutu-
ally-enhancing whole... The Temple complex
perched majestically upon Mount Zion should be
held up as an example of how our artifacts ought
to work in harmony with nature, not destroying
but enhancing God's good creation. (pp 40–41)

Great is the Lord and greatly to be praised in the
city of our God. His holy mountain, beautiful in
elevation is the joy of all the earth, Mount Zion,
in the far north, the city of the great King. Within
her citadels God has made himself known as a
fortress. (Ps 48:1–2)

In the same way that this psalmist looked at Jerusalem in his
day, inspiring the song of Psalm 48, so, too, do Christians gaze in
spiritual vision on the New Jerusalem, inspiring their culture making
today. Significantly, the New Jerusalem is in the shape of a cube—
"its length and width and height are equal" (Rv 21:16)—asserting
that this new city is shaped as the temple of God. It is earth restored
to its original purpose as the dwelling place for God.

And I saw no temple in the city, for its temple is
the Lord God the Almighty and the Lamb. And

the city has no need of sun or moon to shine on
it, for the glory of God gives it light, and its lamp
is the Lamb. (Rv 21:22–23)

The lamp of the New Jerusalem is Jesus Christ, the Lamb of
God, and the light He shines is the glory of God. This is a significant
statement as we consider the effect of mankind's fall into sin on their
creation mandate—to *fill, rule, work, and keep* the earth toward the
Garden-City. The fall infected this mandate but did not remove it.
And more importantly, Jesus Christ came to restore us in the work
of this mandate, His glorification ensuring that it will be completed!

In his book *Creation Regained*, Albert Wolters uses a helpful
analogy to explain this. He likens earth's original creation, and mankind's mandate within it, to a healthy newborn baby. Wolter's explanation of this and then sin's impact bears citing at length:

> In every respect this newborn can be pronounced
> "very good," but this does not mean that change
> is not required. There is something seriously
> wrong if the baby remains in its infancy: it is
> meant to grow, develop, mature into adulthood.
> Suppose now that while the child is still an infant
> it contracts a serious chronic disease for which
> there is no known cure, and that it grows up an
> invalid, the disease wasting its body away. It is
> clear that there are two clearly distinguishable
> processes going on in its body as it approaches
> adolescence: one is the process of maturation
> and growth, which continues in spite of the sick-
> ness and which is natural, normal, and good; the
> other is the progress of the disease, which distorts
> and impairs the healthy functioning of the body.
> Now suppose further that the child has reached
> adolescence when a cure is found for the sickness,
> and it slowly begins to recover its health. As the
> child approaches adulthood there is now a third

process at work in its body: the process of healing, which counteracts and nullifies the action
of the disease and which has no other purpose
than to bring the youth to healthy adulthood, in
which only the normal processes of a sound body
will take place. The child will then be said to be
becoming restored to health after these many
years. (*Creation Regained*, p. 39)

In this analogy, "the ravages of sin do not annihilate the norma-
tive creational development of civilization, but rather are parasitical
upon it" (Wolters). Relatedly, Christians confess that in Jesus Christ,
the cure for the disease of sin has come to our earth! And the medicine of Christ's person and redeeming work restores His people in
their creational mandate—to cultivate the world in fellowship with
God, maturing it toward the Garden City, the New Jerusalem. In this
current age, that "medicine" is administered by Christ's Spirit. He is
Wolter's "third process" at work on earth. And there will come a day,
hallelujah, when the Great Physician Himself—the very medicine we
now receive in "spirit and truth" (Jn 4:24)—will personally return to
earth. Upon that *return*, the disease of sin will be completely erad-
icated from the world by the glory of His presence, bringing full
health, bringing to fulfillment the cultivation of our world, bringing
forth the new heaven and new earth, bringing His people into the
next age of our earth!

Some Implications

Living toward this vision of the New City implies, first of all,
a qualification of the New Testament's denunciation of "worldli-
ness"—i.e., 1 John 3:15:

Do not love the world or the things in the world.
If anyone loves the world, the love of the Father
is not in him.

This command does not steer us away from our creational mandate into a sort of Gnostic, Platonic spirituality. It does not divide the world into the *sacred* and *secular*. As the verse itself implies, it is referring to a relationship with the world that is idolatrous and in place of God. It is treating this world as if this age of it is all there is, hence, living only for "the desires of the flesh and the desires of the eyes and pride in possessions" (1 Jn 3:16). This shortsightedness is forbidden to Christians because we are those called into eternal life. Therefore, we receive all of our world with thanksgiving and seek to cultivate it to the glory of God in preparation for the new earth.

> For everything created by God is good, and nothing is to be rejected if it is received with thanksgiving, for it is made holy by the word of God and prayer. (1 Tm 4:4)

In the creational mandate, Christians embrace all the "spheres" of life in this world (Abraham Kuyper), each with their own authority from and responsibility to God, seeking to cultivate them to His glory: family, politics, business, art, education, journalism, nature, health care, entertainment, sport and, yes, church! All life is holy! There are no sacred and secular jobs. All this world is to be "made holy by the word of God and prayer," cultivating it to God's glory. Reading Scripture in Christ, Christians embrace and live toward the "earthiness" and abundance of Amos' vision of the world:

> "Behold, the days are coming", declares the Lord, "when the plowman shall overtake the reaper and the treader of grapes him who sows the seed; the mountains shall drip sweet wine, and all the hills shall flow with it. I will restore the fortunes of my people Israel, and they shall rebuild the ruined cities and inhabit them; they shall plant vineyards and drink their wine, and they shall make gardens and eat their fruit. I will plant them on their land, and they shall never again be uprooted

out of the land that I have given them." (Am 9:13–15)

To this end, Jesus has come, the Lamb who is the Light of the Holy City. He has come to help mankind fulfill our creational mandate, to unite heaven and earth (Eph 1:9–10) and so develop our world toward its holy eternal state. By His Spirit, we are empowered to cultivate life to God's glory. Jesus' light now is building the new city.

Jesus said,

> Let not your hearts be troubled. Believe in God; believe also in me. In my Father's house are many rooms. If it were not so, would I have told you that I go to prepare a place for you? And if I go and prepare a place for you, I will come again and take you to myself, that where I am you may be also. (Jn. 14:1–3)

This text should not be understood as if Jesus is off in some other celestial universe with hammer in hand, building a mansion in the sky for His people. No! He is building the eternal city now on earth by sending His Spirit to indwell His people. Through their work and in their vision, the "Father's house" (temple), our eternal home is being built, the city Jesus will return to. For that reason, this city comes "down out of heaven from God" (Rv 21:2). The ascended Jesus sends forth His Spirit on earth from the right hand of God and will one day personally return to it. In the Spirit, God's people "see visions and dream dreams" (Acts 2:17), building this world toward the eternal city.

It is important to note that in the Revelation 21 description of the New Jerusalem, the "kings and nations of the earth bring their glory and honor (from this age) into it" (v. 26). There is continuity between the cultivation of creation in this age and that of the age to come. This is the result of the light of the Lamb shining the glory of God in this age now, preparing for the day of *full beam*!

> The city has no need of sun or moon to shine on
> it, for the glory of God gives it light, and its lamp
> is the Lamb. By its light will the nations walk,
> and the kings of the earth will bring their glory in
> to it, and its gates will never be shut by day—and
> there will be no night there. They will bring into
> it the glory and the honor of the nations. (Rv
> 21:23–26)

The honor of the nations is brought into the New Jerusalem—might that be German engineering? Italian wine? French cuisine? New Zealand kiwi? Russian ballet? African drumming? American baseball? We anticipate measures of continuity between this age of the earth and the next because the same Lamb shines the same light of God's glory. Further, in His resurrected body, Jesus bore witness to the continuity between this age and the next. He could be identified by His disciples (but at other times not). He showed them his nail-scarred hands, scars from this age. And as previously stated, another witness is the analogy Jesus taught of the kingdom being in this age of the earth as a child in the womb of her mother. Between the two, there is both continuity and newness. Yet another analogy could be that of a photograph's negative and positive states. In the predigital days, photographs were first taken as negatives—outlines, formations, and shapes were inversely visible on film-strip negatives, formations and shapes that awaited "transfiguration" to radiant color. Even so, this age of the earth, to whatever degree it has been developed, will be transfigured into full color by the glory of the returning Christ.

What about the cultural development work of those outside of Jesus Christ? Will it, too, carry into the New Jerusalem? The Bible gives positive testimony to this.

> The wealth of the sinner is stored up for the righteous. (Prv 13:22)

> God gives wisdom and knowledge and joy to a
> man who is good in His sight; but to the sinner
> He gives the work of gathering and collecting,
> that he may give to him who is good before God.
> (Eccl 2:26)

It does seem to be the case that the righteous in Christ will
inherit even the good culture of the ungodly. This was the case when
the Israelites inherited their promised land. Before settling in that
land, Moses warned them,

> When the Lord your God brings you into the
> land that he swore to your fathers, to Abraham, to
> Isaac, and to Jacob, to give you—with great and
> good cities that you did not build, and houses
> full of all good things that you did not fill, and
> cisterns that you did not dig, and vineyards and
> olive trees that you did not plant—and when you
> eat and are full, then take care lest you forget the
> Lord, who brought you out of the land of Egypt,
> out of the house of slavery. (Dt 6:10–12)

The witness of Scripture affirms the inheritance by the godly of
the good culture of the ungodly. Reading the Bible in Christ, we live
toward that inheritance.

The importance of seeing real continuity between this world
and the next, between the works done now to the glory of God and
the furnishings we will find in the next life, is stated thus by David
Hegeman:

> This gives Christians a profound hope and moti-
> vation for doing culture *now*. While it could be
> argued that doing culture "unto the Lord" should
> be motivation enough, until we grasp the biblical
> teaching that our culturative works will in fact
> have *eternal* significance, our works will always

be undervalued and ignored in favor of more "spiritual" projects. It is only in believing along with Scripture that the best of our art works and our mathematical proofs and our poetry and our scholarly theories will actually contribute to the glory of the life to come that we will lose ourselves from the shallowness and triviality that marks so much of present-day Christendom and strive to take our culturative calling seriously and with all worship and joy. (*Plowing in Hope*, p. 90)

A Biblically-Based Speculative Vision for the Future Age

The Bible makes clear that the new heaven and earth is not the end of human history; rather, it is human history's refreshed beginning. Revelation 22:4–5 describes the servants of God in the New Jerusalem with these words:

> His servants will worship him. They will see his face, and his name will be on their foreheads. And night will be no more. They will need no light of lamp or sun, for the Lord God will be their light, and they will REIGN forever and ever. (Rv 22:4–5)

About this reign, Richard Middleton comments,

> The redeemed human race will once again utilize their God-given power and agency to rule the earth as God intended—a renewal of the human cultural task, but this time without sin. The initial narrative sequence of the biblical story will finally be fulfilled. Far from being the cessation of history, this is history's true beginning, free from the constraints of human violation either vis-à-vis

God, other humans or earth itself. (Middleton, *A New Heaven and a New Earth*)

This explanation of mankind's "reign" accords with Jesus' promised reward to those who have been productive with the gifts of His Spirit in this age:

Well done, good servant, because you have been faithful in a very little, you shall have authority over ten cities. (Luke 19:17)

What might the reign of God's people entail in the new heaven and earth? Reading Scripture in Christ, perhaps our culture making will be not so much *on* earth as *from* earth! If the new earth is then the temple of God restored—the Garden-City in all its beauty, alight with God's glory—might we not parallel humanity's place on that earth with Adam and Eve's in the original garden of Eden? In that garden, Adam and Eve were mandated to *rule, fill, work, and keep*, spreading godly culture into, what was for them, a vast planet we now call Earth. But if the new earth becomes fully the temple of God for the age to come, perhaps mankind's calling will involve the same mandate, but then carried out in, what is for us, our *vast* universe. We have recently come to know so much more about our universe—its size and scope, with millions of stars in each of its millions of galaxies. In the current restrictions of bodily life in this age, this type of cultural mandate seems impossible. But in His resurrected body, Jesus has shown that movements along the dimensions of space and time are radically changed for that body (cf. all the resurrection narratives—"And he vanished from their sight" [Luke 24:31]; "The doors being locked where the disciples were for fear of the Jews, Jesus came and stood among them" [Jn 20:19]; and others). This resurrection reality implies that the redeemed people of God think of our ages of time as *short* and the universe's dimensions of space as *small*, but the callings of God's love as *huge*! Perhaps then, the reign of mankind on the new earth will be from that temple into the universe, cultivating it to God's glory! What adventure that foretells!

C. S. Lewis helps God's people anticipate that future day when, at the end of His Chronicles of Narnia series, he writes these moving words:

> As He (Aslan) spoke, He no longer looked to them like a lion; but the things that began to happen after that were so great and beautiful that I cannot write them. And for us this is the end of all the (Narnian) stories, and we can most truly say that they all lived happily ever after. But for them it was only the beginning of the real story. All their life in this world and all their adventures in Narnia had only been the cover and the title page: now at last they were beginning Chapter One of the Great Story which no one on earth has read: which goes on forever: in which every chapter is better than the one before. (*The Last Battle*, pp 210–211)

"Maranatha—Come, Lord Jesus" (Rv 22:1). Return in your glory to consume and fulfill this age, completing your work of salvation, ushering in the new creation and the call of your people within it.

CONCLUSION

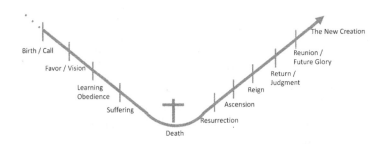

The backbone of this book has been its movement along the Christ plotline, the narrative which Jesus has revealed in history, the narrative which leads to salvation for the people of God and for all of creation. To conclude, let's recognize the importance of this plotline in three areas of the Christian life—reading Scripture, personal counsel, and evangelistic invitation.

Reading Scripture

The grand story of the Bible, Genesis to Revelation, is God's work of restoring creation and building His kingdom on earth to that end. Because this work is done through His Son, Jesus Christ, reading the Bible in Christ leads us to meet Jesus and become part of this grand story. The Christ plotline helps us to find a unity in Scripture amidst all the diversity of its holy writings. It is the central vein running through Scripture, drawing people to Jesus the Messiah, through whom we are drawn into God's grand designs in salvation. The Christ plotline is an organizing principle for the diversity of the Bible's writings—from wisdom to apocalyptic to history to poetry to gospel to epistle. Within each of these types of writing is the story of Jesus—His beginnings (from eternity), obedience, sufferings, death, glorification, reign, judgment, and new creation promises. The Old Testament prefigures this plotline, particularly in the richness of the history of Israel. The Gospels make the plotline most evident, personal and singular in Jesus. The rest of the New Testament grounds believers in the identity and vision of this life in Christ.

To be cognizant of the Christ plotline leads people to meet Jesus through their Bible reading and then become part of His kingdom story. Today, Jesus is the one who is "seated on the throne saying, 'Behold I am making all things new… I am the Alpha and Omega, the beginning and the end. To the thirsty I will give from the spring of the water of life without payment.'" (Rv 21:5–6). The purpose of the Bible, to be clear, is to lead us to this King and drink of His life-giving water. In Jesus' own words, He chastised the Bible readers of His day with this rebuke:

> You search the Scriptures because you think that
> in them you have eternal life; and it is they that
> bear witness about me, yet you refuse to come to
> me that you may have life. (Jn 5:39–40)

May that never be said of our reading of Scripture. As Eliza Hewitt prayed in 1887 (highlighting her third stanza):

More about Jesus would I know, more of His grace to others show;
More of His saving fullness see, more of His love who died for me.

Refrain: More, more about Jesus, more, more about Jesus;
More of His saving fullness see, more
of His love who died for me.

More about Jesus let me learn, more of His holy will discern;
Spirit of God, my teacher be, showing the
things of Christ to me. (Refrain)

More about Jesus, in His Word, holding communion with my Lord;
Hearing His voice in every line, making each
faithful saying mine. (Refrain)

More about Jesus on His throne, riches in glory all His own;
More of His kingdom's sure increase; more of
his coming, Prince of Peace. (Refrain)

Personal Counsel

In the current field of therapeutic counseling, a recently developed method is called narrative counseling. Central to narrative therapy is the idea that throughout life, people create "narratives" to interpret the events that happen to them, stories that have a profound effect on how we live our lives. Such narratives may include negative stories such as "I'm a bad person," "I'm not worthy of having a loving relationship," "I will not succeed in life." In this form of therapy, people become active agents cultivating a different "story" to live into, one of love and happiness. (Hence the value of *fairy tales*…"and they lived happily ever after.")

Here's the good news of the gospel: God, our Maker and Redeemer, has given us His saving eternal narrative to live in and into! It is in His Son, Jesus the Christ. It is the Christ plotline. By the Christ narrative, Christians are grounded in an identity to lead them through the wilderness of this age.

> For me to live is Christ, and to die is gain. (Phil 1:21)

This is the Christian identity wherein we interpret all the vicissitudes of life. Living in Christ means that we have been divinely born again, set in God's favor, and called to be His servants in this age. But like Jesus, it, too, means that we must learn obedience, gain wisdom, and experience suffering and pain. Life is difficult. It brings much temptation and sorrow. The Christ plotline brings meaning in such trial. It brings us to Jesus—the "narrow gate" and the "hard way that leads to life" (Mt 7:13–14). In John Bunyan's *Pilgrim's Progress*, Christian had to go through the Slough of Despond, past Giant Despair, face the temptations of Vanity Fair, and discern beyond Worldly Wiseman in order to make it to the Celestial City. Grounded in the Christ plotline, today's pilgrims learn to "keep in step with the Spirit" (Gal 5:16), walking in fellowship with Jesus, gaining His wisdom and holiness in the trials and temptations of life.

Thus, the deepest passion in the apostle Paul's heart is to "know Christ" (Phil 3:8):

> The power of His resurrection, sharing his suffer-ings, in becoming like him in his death, so that by any means possible I may attain the resurrection from the dead. Not that I have already obtained this or am already made perfect, but I press on to make it my own, because Christ Jesus has made me his own...forgetting what lies behind and straining forward to what lies ahead, I press on toward the goal for the prize of the upward call of God in Christ Jesus. (Phil 3:10–14)

That is Christ-narrative living! The death-to-life plotline is lived throughout life taken as a whole but also day-to-day as we give up our will for Christ's and therein experience true abundant eternal life.

> For me to live is Christ, **and to die is gain.** (emphasis mine)

The Christian never forgets where the Christ plotline's journey heads—into full union with the glory of Jesus and the new creation He has begun wherein His people reign to God's glory. That story is God's narrative therapy and ongoing counsel for our lives! In it, a Christian is grafted and grounded.

Evangelistic Invitation

The Christ plotline contains within it a fresh call for the ministry of evangelism, one with an eschatological vision. With the increasingly rapid changes of our day, technologically and socially, a question latent on the hearts of all people is, where are things heading in this age? What does the future hold?. The message of the Bible, as revealed in Jesus, has an exciting vision for the future of this world, one that each person is invited to become part of! In Christ, God is building His kingdom on earth, a kingdom which will fill the new earth, a kingdom you are invited to enter and then live toward, knowing that your life toward that kingdom today will bear its fulfillment in that future day!

This vision invites people to be part of a new breed of humanity in Jesus Christ. It invites people to become part of the next age of this earth. This vision even embraces a call to explore and develop our entire universe! This is a vision that redeems the narratives of science, even the narratives of evolution. Given the world's current embrace of science and evolution, this invitation can speak to the modern mind—not presenting a Christian faith juxtaposed to science but one that redeems its insights. It is the call to become part of a new breed of humanity; the call to be part of the new creation's story. The call to live with this vision in Christ is an evangelistic call that needs issuing in our day.

Too much yet, our evangelistic call, particularly in Protestant circles, is centered on reconciliation with God, dealing with the issues of sin and guilt. Not that this is not central to the Christian life. It is, and the writings of the New Testament make that clear. But reconciliation with God through Jesus Christ is not the end of the gospel; it is the means to become part of God's greater vision for the earth and for one's own future in it. "The time is fulfilled and the Kingdom of God is at hand" was Jesus' seminal proclamation (Mk 1:15). To be part of the kingdom, yes, one must repent to become a follower of Jesus (Mk 1:17), so indeed the realities of personal sin and guilt before a holy God must be faced and renounced in sorrow. Thanks be to God that Jesus' death in history is the assurance of that needed forgiveness. But once forgiven, the Christian life is about kingdom living! Jesus has reconciled His people to God so that through them, heaven might grow on earth—the future has arrived; let's live in it! Jesus did not come to bring mankind to some otherworldly heaven; He came to bring heaven on earth—through a new mankind, reborn with His Spirit.

This evangelistic vision leads us to embrace our world for God's glory, engaging culture and society in His truth. It leads us to care for our environment in the name of Jesus. It leads us to transform society toward justice and human flourishing. Jesus is God's shalom, and that shalom is all encompassing. He brings reconciliation with our Maker so that we might become His forever people living toward the new heaven and earth. This vision in Christ is God's gospel for our world, and its invitation must be made known.

Behold, I am making all things new (Rv 21:5),

says Jesus seated on His throne.

> The Spirit and the Bride say, "Come." And let the one who hears say, "Come." And let the one who is thirsty come; let the one who desires take the water of life without price. (Rv 22:17)

ACKNOWLEDGMENTS

First, I want to thank my wife, Karen, with whom I have the privilege to regularly read, discuss, and apply the Bible. Her faith and daily prayers inspire mine. I am grateful for her review and comments on this book.

I want to thank my mother, Tine, who introduced me to a love for the stories of the Bible. I remember being captivated as a child by the resilience of Joseph and his story. Only the Lord knows all the ways that such fascination eventually led me to Jesus and life in Him.

I want to thank my five children for their love for the Bible, having listened to it each day in their years at home, now leading to their love for the Living Word today. Some of them, too, have given valuable input on this book.

Dr. S. Joshua Swamidass and Jon Garvey gave helpful assistance for the appendix of this book. Their review of it and suggestions were very much appreciated. I want to also thank my friends, Dr. Carl Toren, Pastor Jon Dennis and Steve Ahrenholtz, for their reviews and comments on this book. It is through Dr. Toren that I was invited to teach at Onesimus Nesib Seminary in Ethiopia in 2005. There the seeds for this book were planted.

So I, too, want to thank the students of Onesimus Nesib Seminary who, in 2005, enthusiastically received the teaching of this book and encouraged me toward its further development. It is my sincere hope to revisit them in the near future and present copies to them.

APPENDIX

Reading in Christ Biblical Accounts of Human Origins

Since Jesus taught his disciples to read Scripture in the light of who He is (Luke. 24:44–47), may this not impact also the way we read the biblical accounts of human origins? Jesus is the new humanity set among mankind to transform us into eternal beings fit for a new earth. In the words of C. S. Lewis, he has come to "change us from being creatures of God to being sons of God" (*Mere Christianity,* p. 220). In this calling of bringing eternal life on earth, Jesus is identified as the "Second Adam" (Rom. 5:12–15; 1 Cor. 15:45–49). Here then is a possible way to understand the biblical accounts of human origins Christocentrically and in the light of some of the latest insights of science.

Genesis 2:4–25 is the story of the formation and calling of the first Adam. Clearly it is a creation story distinct from Genesis 1 and can be understood sequentially from it. Genesis 1:1–2:3 is a broad sweeping account of the creation of our entire universe by the Almighty God, "Elohim," including the creation of "humanity" in the broadest sense of that word on the sixth day of creation (Gen. 1:26–27). The phrase, "broadest sense of humanity," refers to different ways that "humans" can be defined.

In his book, *The Genealogical Adam and Eve*, Joshua Swamidass, a computational biologist and physician, writes:

> There are many ways to define *human* in science. The particulars of each of these definitions are subject to substantial debate and revision. Nonetheless, we can identify several markers in history that may be important starting points from which to build more careful definitions:
>
> 1. Six thousand to twelve thousand years ago, when permanent settlements associated with agriculture arise across the globe,
> 2. About fifty thousand to one hundred thousand years ago, with the rise of *behaviorally modern humans*, a chronological subset of *Homo sapiens* as a whole,
> 3. About one hundred fifty thousand to three hundred thousand years ago, with the rise of *anatomically modern humans*, also known as *Homo sapiens*,
> 4. About five hundred thousand to seven hundred thousand years ago, with the common ancestor of Neanderthals, *Homo sapiens*, Denisovans, and other hominins no longer among us,
> 5. About 2 million years ago, with the rise of *Homo* genus, including many hominins no longer found among us. (*The Genealogical Adam and Eve*, p. 103)

Returning to the Genesis 1:1–2:3 account of creation, the creation of humanity described in 1:26–27 can refer to humanity in its totality in all of the above definitions, leading to present-day humanity. (Note: a sixth definition of human could also be identified, having been introduced into the story of our world about 2,000 years ago in the person of Jesus, who Christians confess to be the true, pure human and who leads His people into that state of being).

In the Genesis 1:1–2:3 overarching account of creation, humans are created in the image of God to rule on earth as Elohim's vice regents. This lends credence to the best understanding of the Genesis 1 creation account as God's work of temple-building and dedication, the temple being a home for His presence. His final act of creation, therefore, on the sixth day is to place his image in the temple (as is customary in any temple construction and dedication), that image being mankind to rule in God's stead and in relationship with Him.

Thereafter comes Genesis 2:4–25, a very different story of creation, this time by the Covenant God, "Yahweh," translated the "Lord" God. This is the account of Yahweh's creation of the "first Adam" and the special garden in Eden into which he is placed. In light of who Jesus is (the "second Adam"), might we not best understand the creation of the first Adam (the forefather of all humanity alive today), likewise as a unique human created among a broader "type" of humanity? In his creation, the First Adam is "breathed into the breath of life and becomes a living creature" (Gen. 2:7), a foreshadow of Jesus' unique conception by the power of the Holy Spirit (Luke 1:35). Jesus is truly a human fully "alive!"

As "living creatures," therefore, Adam and Eve (his helpmate of one substance with him) possess eternal life in holy fellowship with God. In Adam, a new line of humanity is being formed, a line defined Godward. They, like Jesus, are a new breed of humanity in their day. Their possession of holy fellowship with God, however, is yet in an unconfirmed state. God places Adam and Eve in the specially prepared Garden of Eden (a "Holy of Holies" in the creation temple) to test their love for Him and their obedience to the eternal godly life (The life C. S. Lewis refers to as "Zoe"—*Mere Christianity*, p. 221) in which they were uniquely created. Had they remained faithful in this test of love (as the second Adam does in His testing—Matt. 4:1–11), Adam and Eve's calling in confirmed eternal life would have been, in their work and witness, like that of Jesus'—"changing creatures of God (i.e., other 'types' of humanity) into the sons of God."

This Christocentric reading of Adam's origin and calling incorporates insights consistent with findings of recent science. Humankind today can trace our identity *genetically* to a distant past—the great apes, hominids, Neanderthal man, etc.—up to 300,000 years ago. Humankind today can also trace our identity *genealogically* to an historical Adam and Eve, one human couple from as recent as 6,000–10,000 years ago and from whom all humankind living today has genealogical descent.

Swamidass introduces this helpful distinction between genetic and genealogical inheritance in his aforementioned book and in a related paper, "The Overlooked Science of Genealogical Ancestry" (March 2018, *Perspectives on Science and Christian Faith Publications*, volume 70, Issue 1 // c.f. also https://asa3.org/ASA/PSCF/2018/PSCF3-18Swamidass.pdf). He writes:

> It cannot be overemphasized that genetic ancestry is not genealogical ancestry. Genealogical ancestry traces the reproductive origin of people, matching the common use of "ancestor," "descendent," "parent," and "child." In contrast, genetic ancestry has a much more exotic meaning, tracing the origin of stretches of DNA... Consider a child's father and grandfather. They are both fully the child's genealogical ancestors. However, they are only partially the child's genetic ancestors, approximately 1/2 and 1/4, respectively. The same is true of the child's mother and grandmothers. Genetic ancestry continues to dilute each generation: 1/8, 1/16, 1/32...to a number so small it is unlikely a descendent has any genetic material from a specific ancestor. Which type of ancestry is most relevant to our central question, could all humans "descend" from any individual couple? In non-technical discussion, questions about "descent" are questions about genealogical ancestry. DNA is a recent discovery,

and genetic ancestry is a very new way of looking at the world. In the genomic age our tendency is to start with genetic ancestry, but we must look to genealogic science to answer genealogical questions. ("The Overlooked Science of Genealogical Ancestry," p. 3–4)

Using genealogical science, the computational biologist, Swamidass, cites calculations that estimate that a universal ancestral couple (i.e., an Adam and Eve) arises in quite recent human history. He writes:

"The *most recent universal genealogical ancestor* of all living humans might have been situated as recently as 3,000 years ago. We can build intuition about this by counting back generations while simultaneously tracking the total population and the number of ancestors we expect from a naïve calculation. First, we have two parents, then four grandparents, then eight great-grandparents. The number of ancestors appears to increase *exponentially* as we go back, however the number of people in past generations either stays comparatively *constant* in much of paleo-history or *decreases exponentially* over the last 10,000 years. How is this possible? Very quickly, all our genealogies begin to "collapse" by sharing more and more ancestors. The first genealogical ancestor appears quickly, in just a few thousand years in realistic simulations. (p. 7)*

---

* The matter of how it is geographically possible for the entire globe of present-day humanity to genealogically descend from one universal ancestral couple is a subject covered in Swamidass' book and a topic beyond the scope of this appendix.

This calculation accords with the biblical statement in Acts 17:26, "And he [God] made from one man every nation of mankind to live on the face of the earth." Adam and Eve are every present-day human's genealogical parents. (In Swamidaas' model this would be the case minimally from the year AD 1 on—*The Genealogical Adam and Eve*, p. 26, 31). Every modern human's family tree goes back to them, even if they are as recent as 6,000 years ago. Of course, Adam and Eve could be more ancient too; science does not tell us when they lived.

A word about the prominence and significance of biblical genealogies is here in order. Both the Old and New Testaments feature numerous genealogies. As Swamidass notes, with our modern scientific mindset, we tend to read these genealogies through a genetic lens. But that is not a biblical and theological understanding. Theologically, biblical genealogies refer primarily to spiritual identity, not genetic identity.

Yes, there is physical descent from ancestors, but as Swamidass states, genetic inheritance from a specific ancestor is essentially indiscernible. Biblically, descent is a matter of spiritual identity. In fact, in the genealogy of the Gospel of Luke, chapter 3:23–38, it states that Adam is a "son of God" (v. 38). Obviously, this does not refer to a genetic inheritance. Adam, like the rest of the "sons" in this genealogy, has a spiritual identity through his genealogical heritage, called to be God's vice regent on earth. This genealogical spiritual identity is entered through the Word of God. It comes with God's calling on that person's life, a calling through the agency of His Spirit (the "breath of God;" Gen. 2:7). Because we are each descendant of Adam and Eve, that called identity is upon all of present-day humanity. In this sense, then, all human descendants of Adam and Eve are inheritors of that same spiritual identity as God's Word declares it.

Putting together these realities in a very fundamental manner, we might distinguish between "Biological Humanity" (earliest bipedal hominids 300,000 years ago, perhaps longer), "Psychological Humanity" (50,000–100,000 years ago, perhaps longer—"humans" begin tool-making, cave-painting), and then the creation of "Covenantal Humanity," Adam and Eve as described in Scripture (around 10,000 years ago)—unique, God-breathed, God-called, modern humanity—originally created in holiness through the Spirit of eternal life, the ancestors of all present-day humanity.**

Here then is a plausible scenario reading Scripture historically and Christocentrically and considering insights from science:

It is inconsequential whether Adam and Eve were created out of an existing breed of humanity or created "de novo," but when historically created they were breathed into by God's Spirit and so uniquely set apart as humans holy unto God ("Covenantal Humanity"), identified spiritually as a "son of God" by His Word and Spirit. In Adam and Eve, a new breed was created in the story of humanity, just as today a new breed of humanity has been recreated in Jesus Christ. Had Adam and Eve remained faithful in godly life, their calling would have been to bring that holy eternal life to other breeds of humanity who were at that time mere "creatures of God needing to become sons of God" (Lewis).

Through their work and witness, God's Spirit would have been ministering eternal life through them, just as He does today through Jesus and His followers. In conjunction with that calling, Adam and Eve too would have extended the goodness, beauty, and flourish of the Garden of Eden throughout the earth.

Spiritually, to bring eternal life to the rest of "humanity" on earth would have meant revealing the self-giving creative character of

---

** In God's economy of time, "one day is as a thousand years and a thousand years as one day" (2 Pet. 3:8). So measures of time should only enhance appreciation of an artist's work, as we do with the Sistine Chapel which took Michelangelo four years to paint! Gargantuan measures of time and space only help Christians appreciate the immensity of God their Creator and His redeeming love of Jesus Christ—"so that Christ may dwell in our hearts through faith—that we, being rooted and grounded in love, may have strength to comprehend with all the saints what is the breadth and length and height and depth and to know the love of Christ that surpasses knowledge that we may be filled with all the fullness of God" (Eph. 3:17–19). Further, if geological time is billions of years, then present-day human history is relatively "one day," a blink of the eye. Salvation history, beginning with Adam and Eve, through to Jesus Christ, through to the present day is truly "one day." Our modern human history quite literally then is Christ's story.

God, inviting others to know and receive that breath of life and then live in relationship with God. In this, Adam and Eve would be calling humanity from a creaturely, natural, and mortal state of being to the higher state of sonship, just as Jesus does today.

But tragically, Adam and Eve chose to leave that life of God and their calling from Him. In their fall into sin (Gen. 3), they chose a life of self-centeredness, distrust in God, and disobedience. They chose to rebel against the very nature and person of God. Therein came their death—immediate spiritual death (Eph. 2:1)—and eventual physical death (their forfeiture of godly immortality would presumably have also involved the forfeiture of a related translation of their physical selves after their time of testing, even as the Lord Jesus was physically translated in the resurrection after his obedience unto death on the cross).

They too lost their original calling among other types of humanity, at least until God, in mercy, came to them again, asking, "Where are you" (Gen. 3:9)? With that question, God was initiating a plan of salvation and restoration through the offspring of Adam and Eve, one fulfilled in Christ Jesus.

Thus, Adam and Eve were exiled from the Garden. We then read in the biblical story of their son, Cain, that he "settled in the land of Nod" and "knew his wife who conceived and bore Enoch" (Gen. 4:16–17). Quite plausibly, it is at this point in time that Adam and Eve's descendants begin a life interbreeding with other "types" of humanity then existent (hence humanity's genetic heritage dating beyond our genealogical heritage).

Genesis 6:2 may also refer to this interbreeding—the "sons of God" taking as wives the "daughters of men." As that interbreeding continued, it was not long before all humankind became genealogical descendants of Adam and Eve, thereby inheriting their spiritual identity.

As genealogical descendants, the sons and daughters of Adam and Eve have a threefold inheritance: their Covenantal identity through God's Word—called as vice regents in an original relationship and holy fellowship with God; their spiritual fallen condition (Rom. 5:12), having rejected holy fellowship with God, falling into a life of self-centeredness and death; and a complex genetic heritage through the interbreeding that occurred among other types of humanity.

This accounts for our current spiritual condition as modern humans. We search for meaning because by His breath, "God has put eternity into man's heart" (Eccles. 3:11). We have capacities for self-giving love yet are indifferent and struggle to do so. We innately value beauty and goodness and discern "right and wrong," "better and worse." But these categories of human experience ultimately have no meaning apart from our descent from Adam, and his original spiritual identity as a "son of God," living in holy fellowship with God. Likewise, we intuitively experience death as an enemy (1 Cor. 15:26), not merely as part of the "circle of life" (*"Do not go gentle into that good night…rage, rage against the dying of the light"—Dylan Thomas*). As genealogical descendants of Adam and Eve, people today are God's fullest expression of human beings (apart from Jesus—the higher, true human—and those "in Christ"), yet we are fallen in sin.

Thus, it was not until the special formation of the Second Adam, the eternal Son conceived in Mary's womb by the power of the Holy Spirit, that God's original design to build a holy humanity on a holy earth was reestablished. In Jesus, then, we begin a life restored to our original callings in God in fellowship with His Holy Spirit. Breathed into by the Spirit, the new humanity is called to manifest to others the self-giving love and holy nature of God (revealed most clearly in the historical crucifixion of Jesus) and to cultivate the goodness of Eden, developing the world to His glory with creativity and industry.

In the meaning of Jesus' person and life, this then is one possible way of understanding the first chapters of the Bible, chapters included in Jesus' statement, "Everything must be fulfilled that is written about me in the Law of Moses" (Luke 24:44).

SELECTED
BIBLIOGRAPHY

Bunyan, John. *Pilgrim's Progress*. Chicago: Moody Publishers, 1971.

Chesterton, Gilbert K. *The Everlasting Man*. London: Hodder & Stoughton, 1925.

D'Souza, Dinesh. *What's so Great About Christianity*. Washington, DC: Regnery Publishing, 2007.

English Standard Version. Wheaton, IL: Crossway Bibles, a division of Good News Publishers, 2001.

Feddes, David. "The World Changer." *Back to God Hour*. Grand Rapids, MI: Reframe Media, 2002.

Garvey, Jon. "A Biblical Theology of People Outside the Garden." peacefulscience.org. May 14, 2020.

Hegeman, David B. *Plowing in Hope*. Moscow, ID: Canon Press, 1999.

"Heidelberg Catechism." Grand Rapids, MI: *Faith Alive Christian Resources*. CRC Publications, 1988 (Original, 1563).

Jones, Douglas, and Douglas Wilson. *Angels in the Architecture*. Moscow, ID: Canon Press, 1998.

Kennedy, D. James, and Jerry Newcombe. *What If Jesus Had Never Been Born*. Nashville, TN: Thomas Nelson, 1994.

Kristoff, Nicholas. "Why 2018 Was the Best Year Ever." *New York Times*, January 5, 2019.

Lewis, Clive S. *Mere Christianity*. San Francisco, CA: HarperCollins, 2001 (Originally, 1952).

———. The Chronicles of Narnia. Francisco, CA: HarperCollins, (Originally, 1956).

Middleton, Richard. *A New Heaven and a New Earth*. Ada, MI: Baker Publishing, 2014.

————. "A New Heaven and a New Earth: The Case for a Holistic Reading of the Biblical Story of Redemption"—paper, *Journal for Christian Theological Research*, 2006.

Morrow, Jeff. "Creation as Temple-Building and Work as Liturgy in Genesis 1–3." moseseditor.blogspot.com, 2012.

New International Version. Grand Rapids, MI: Zondervan, 1978.

Pinker, Steven. *The Better Angels of our Nature*. New York, NY: Viking, Penguin Group, 2011.

Sliker, David. "One of the Most Fascinating Things to Ponder About Jesus." Facebook post, May 17, 2020.

Swamidass, S. Joshua. The Genealogical Adam and Eve. Downers Grove, IL: InterVarsity Press, 2019.

Walton, John. *The Lost World of Genesis One: Ancient Cosmology and the Origins Debate*. Downers Grove, IL: InterVarsity Press, 2010.

Wolters, Albert M. *Creation Regained: Biblical Basics for a Reformational Worldview*. Grand Rapids, MI: Eerdmans Publishing, 1985.

Wright, N. T. *Surprised by Hope: Rethinking Heaven, the Resurrection, and the Mission of the Church*. San Francisco, CA: HarperCollins, 2008.

ABOUT THE AUTHOR

Rev. Heino A. Blaauw is an ordained Minister of Word and Sacrament with the Reformed Church in America. He has Bachelor's degrees in theology and psychology, along with a Master's of Divinity degree from Tyndale Seminary, Toronto. He has pastored churches in Canada and the United States, including a church-plant in Canada. He has been a guest professor at Onesimus Nesib Seminary in Ethiopia and teaches part time at South Suburban Community College, South Holland, Illinois. He currently serves as a chaplain with Providence Life Services of Chicagoland where he preaches, teaches, prays, and counsels.

CPSIA information can be obtained
at www.ICGtesting.com
Printed in the USA
BVHW061502220222
629766BV00001B/94